70 DAYS FASTING AND PRAYER PROGRAMME
ENGLISH EDITION

PRAYERS THAT BRING UNPARALLELED FAVOUR

DR. D. K. OLUKOYA
General Overseer
MFM MINISTRIES, LAGOS, NIGERIA

(Dr. D. K. Olukoya)
© 2015 A.D.

A publication of:

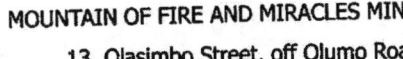
MOUNTAIN OF FIRE AND MIRACLES MINISTRIES
13, Olasimbo Street, off Olumo Road,
(By UNILAG Second Gate), Onike, Iwaya
P. O. Box 2990, Sabo, Yaba, Lagos.
E-Mail: mfmhqworldwide@mountainoffire.org
Web-site: www.mountainoffire.org

All rights reserved. No part of this publication may be reproduced, stored in a retrieval system, or be transmitted, in any form, or by any means, mechanical, electronic, photocopying or otherwise without the prior written consent of the publisher. It is protected under the copyright laws.

ISBN 978-0692496602

I salute my wonderful wife, Pastor Shade, for her invaluable support in the ministry. I appreciate her unquantifiable support in the book ministry as the cover designer, art editor and art adviser

All Scripture are quoted from the King James Version of the Bible

PREFACE

"O Thou that hearest prayer, unto thee shall all flesh come" (Ps 65:2).

We give all the glory to the Lord for what He has been doing with our annual Seventy days prayer and fasting programme. The Lord has used the programme to: ignite the fire of revival in thousands of lives, put stubborn pursuers to flight, produce prayer eagles, open chapters of prosperity for many, confuse satanic dribblers and put the enemies' gear in reverse. Prayer is of great value in turbulent and non-turbulent situations. Prayer is a necessity not an option.

"Howbeit this kind goeth not out but by PRAYER AND FASTING" (Matt 17:21).

Some mountains will not fall unless they are bombarded with the artillery of prayer and fasting.

The weapon of prayer and fasting have been known to do wonders when other methods have failed. In addition, some breakthroughs are impossible unless there is regular, consistent, concerted, constant bombardment of prayers. The prayer points for this year's programme have been specially vomited by the Holy Ghost to bring salvation, deliverance and healing of the spirit, soul and body to God's people. Pray them with determination, pray them with aggression, pray them with violence in your spirit, pray them with violent faith, pray them with great expectation and your life will never remain the same. The God who answereth by fire will surely answer you, in Jesus' name.

Your friend in the school of prayer,
Dr. D. K. OLUKOYA

DEVOTIONAL SONGS

THE BLOOD HAS NEVER LOST ITS POWER

MRS. C. H MORRIS

O SAVIOUR, BLESS US ERE WE GO (8.8.8.D)

St. Matthias
Williams H. Monk, 1861

THERE'S A STRANGER AT THE DOOR (7.3.7.3.7.7.7.3)

JONATHAN B. ATCHINSON   EDWIN O. EXCELL

THE CHURCH HAS WAITED LONG (D.S.M. & Ref)

E.J Hopkins.

O JESUS, I HAVE PROMISED

AURELIA
D. 7s. 6s.

HYMN NUMBER 5 - MUSIC

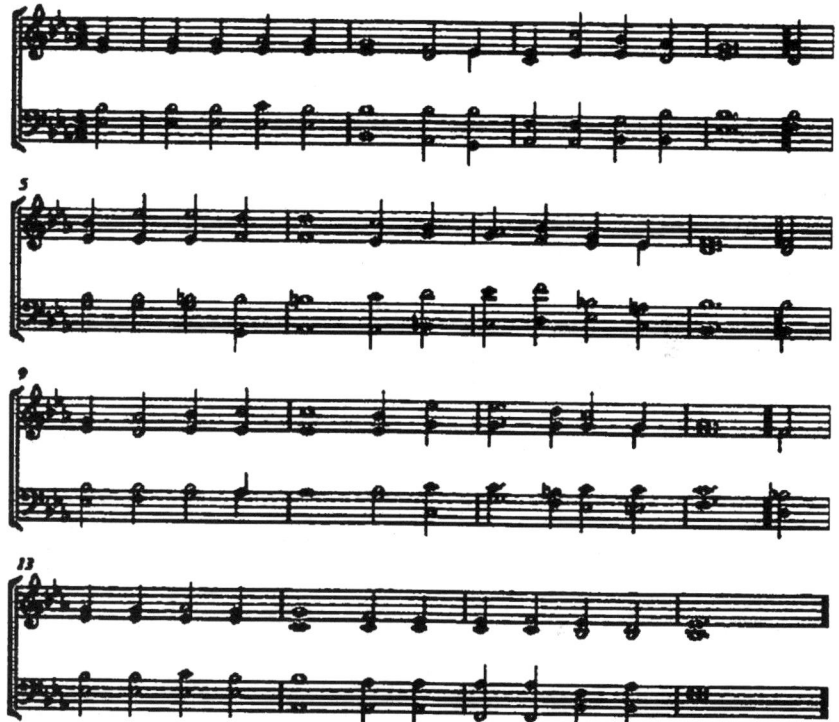

HEAR THE FOOTSTEPS OF JESUS

Wilt Thou Be Made Whole

HYMN FOR THE VIGIL

W. J. K.   Wm. J. Kirkpatrick

MFM 2015 SEVENTY DAYS PRAYER & FASTING

HYMN NUMBER 1
THE BLOOD HAS NEVER LOST ITS POWER

1. *f* In the misty days of yore
   Jesus' precious blood had pow'r
   mf E'en the thief upon the cross to save;
   Like a bird his spirit flies
   To its home in Paradise,
   Thro' the pow'r of Calv'ry's crimson wave.

Chorus
   f And the blood has never lost its pow'r,
   ff No, never, no, never,
   mf Jesus' blood avails for sin forever,
   f And will never lose its pow'r.

2. *p* I was lost and stepped in guilt,
   But the blood for sinners spilt
   mf Wash'd away my sins and set me free;
   Now and evermore the same,
   Praise, O praise His holy name!
   Will the cleansing stream availing be.

3. *mp* God in mercy asks you why,
   p Brother sinner, will you die
   mf When such full redemption He provides?
   You have but to look and live,
   Life eternal He will give,
   For the pow'r of Calv'ry still abides

4. *mf* Bring your burdens, come today,
   Turn from all your sins away,
   He can fully save and sanctify;
   From the wrath to come now flee,
   Let your name recorded be
   With the blood-washed, and redeem'd on high.

   Mrs C. H. Morris

HYMN NUMBER 2
FOR MY SAKE AND THE GOSPEL'S GO (8.78.7.D.)
For my sake and the gospel. Mark 8:35

1. *f* 'For my sake and the Gospel's, go
   And tell Redemption's story,'
   cr His heralds answer, 'Be it so,
   f And Thine, Lord, all the glory!'
   mf They preach His Birth, His Life, His Cross,
   The love of His Atonement
   For Whom they count the world but loss,
   f His rising, His Enthronement

2. *f* Hark, hark, the trump of Jubilee
   Proclaims to every nation,
   cr From pole to pole, by land and sea,
   Glad tidings of salvation:
   p As nearer draws the day of doom,
   While still the battle rages,
   f The Heavenly Dayspring through the gloom
   Breaks on the night of ages

3. *f* Still on and on the anthems spread
   Of Hallelujah voices,
   cr In concert with the holy Dead
   The warrior Church rejoices;
   Their snow-white robes are washed in Blood,
   Their golden harps are ringing;
   ff Earth and the Paradise of God
   One Triumph-song are singing

MFM 2015 SEVENTY DAYS PRAYER & FASTING

4. *f* He comes, Whose Advent Trumpet drowns
The last of Time's evangels,
Emmanuel crown'd with many crowns,
The Lord of Saints and Angels:

cr O Life, Light, Love, the great I AM,
Truine, Who changest never,
ff The Throne of God and of the Lamb
Is Thine, and Thine for ever!

E. H. Bickersleth

HYMN NUMBER 3
O SAVIOUR, BLESS US ERE WE GO
For the Lord shall be thine everlasting light. Isa. 60:20

1. *mf* O Saviour, bless us ere we go;
Thy Word into our minds instill,
And make our lukewarm hearts to glow
With lowly love and fervent will.
cr Through life's long day and death's dark night,
p O gentle Jesus, be our Light.

2. *mp* The day is done, its hours have run,
And Thou hast taken count of all,
The scanty triumphs grace hath won,
The broken vow, the frequent fall.

3. *mf* Forgive us, Lord, yea, give us joy,
Sweet fear, and sober liberty,
And loving hearts without alloy
That only long to be like Thee.

4. *mp* Labour is sweet, for Thou hast toil'd,
And care is light, for Thou hast cared;
Let not our works with self be soil'd,
Nor in unsimple ways ensnared.

5. *mp* For all we love, the poor, the sad,
The sinful, unto Thee we call;
O let Thy mercy make us glad:
Thou art our Saviour, and our all.

6. *mf* O Saviour, bless us; night is come;
Thy holy presence with us be;
Good angels watch about our home,
And we are one day nearer Thee.

F. W. Faber

HYMN NUMBER 4
THERE'S A STRANGER AT THE DOOR (7.37.3.7.7.7.3)
Behold I stand at the door, and knock Rev. 3:20

1. *mp* There's a Stranger at the door,
Let Him in;
He has been there oft before,
Let Him in;
Let Him in, ere He is gone,
Let Him in, the Holy One,
cr Jesus Christ, the Father's Son,
Let Him in.

2. *mp* Open now to Him your heart,
Let Him in;
di If you wait He will depart,
Let Him in;
cr Let Him in, He is your Friend,
He your soul will sure defend,
He will keep you to the end,
Let Him in.

MFM 2015 SEVENTY DAYS PRAYER & FASTING

3. *mp* Hear you now His loving voice?
   Let Him in;
   Now, oh, now make Him your choice,
   Let Him in;
   He is standing at your door,
   cr Joy to you He will restore,
   And His name you will adore,
   Let Him in.

4. *mf* Now admit the heav'nly Guest,
   Let Him in;
   He will make for you a feast,
   Let Him in;
   cr He will speak your sins forgiven.
   And when earth ties all are riven,
   He will take you home to heaven,
   Let Him in.

J. Atchiison

HYMN NUMBER 5
THE CHURCH HAS WAITED LONG (D.S.M. & Ref)
Surely, I come quickly Rev. 22:20

1. *mp* The Church has waited long,
   Her absent Lord to see,
   And still in loneliness she waits,
   A friendless stranger she.
   Age after age has gone,
   Sun after sun has set,
   And still of her dear Lord bereft,
   She weeps a mourner yet.
   Come then, Lord Jesus, come!

2. *mp* Saint after saint on earth
   Has lived, and loved, and died;
   p And as they left us one by one,
   We laid them side by side;
   pp We laid them down to sleep,
   But not in hope forlorn;
   cr We laid them but to ripen there,
   Till the last glorious morn.
   Come then, Lord Jesus, come!

3. The serpent's brood increase,
   The powers of hell grow bold,
   The conflict thickens, faith is low,
   And love is waxing cold.
   cr How long, O Lord our God,
   Holy, and true, and good,
   Wilt Thou not judge Thy suffering Church,
   Her sighs, and tears, and blood?
   Come then, Lord Jesus, come!

4. *mf* We long to hear Thy voice,
   To see Thee face to face,
   To share Thy crown and glory then,
   As now we share Thy grace.
   f Come, Lord, and wipe away
   The curse, the sin, the stain,
   And make this blighted world of ours
   Thine own fair world again.
   Come then, Lord Jesus, come!

Dr. H. Bonar

HYMN NUMBER 6
O JESUS I HAVE PROMISED (7.6.7.6 D)
If any man serve me, let him follow me (John 12:26)

1. *mp* O Jesus, I have promised
   To serve Thee to the end;
   Be Thou forever near me,
   My Master and my Friend:
   I shall not fear the battle
   If Thou art by my side,
   Nor wander from the pathway
   If Thou wilt be my guide.

2. O let me feel Thee near me,
   The world is ever near;
   I see the sights that dazzle,
   The tempting sounds I hear:
   di My foes are ever near me,
   Around me and within;
   cr But, Jesus, draw Thou nearer,
   And shield my soul from sin.

MFM 2015 SEVENTY DAYS PRAYER & FASTING

3. *p* O let me hear Thee speaking
In accents clear and still,
Above the storms of passion,
The murmurs of selfwill,
cr O speak to reassure me,
To chasten or control;
O speak, and make me listen,
Thou Guardian of my soul.

4. *mf* O Jesus, Thou hast promised
To all who follow Thee,
That where Thou art in glory,
There shall Thy servant be;
And, Jesus, I have promised
To serve Thee to the end;
O give me grace to follow,
My Master and my Friend.

5. *p* O let me see Thy footmarks
And in them plant mine own;
My hope to follow duly
Is in Thy strength alone,
O guide me, call me, draw me,
Uphold me to the end;
And then in heaven receive me,
My Saviour and my Friend.

HYMN FOR THE VIGIL
HEAR THE FOOTSTEPS OF JESUS (13.13.12.12 & Ref)
For I am the Lord that healeth thee (Exod. 15:26)

1. *f* Hear the footsteps of Jesus,
He is now passing by,
Bearing balm for the wounded,
Healing all who apply;
As He spake to the suff'rer
Who lay at the pool,
He is saying this moment,
"Wilt thou be made whole?"

Refrain
mf Wilt thou be made whole?
Wilt thou be made whole?
P Oh come, weary suff'rer,
Oh come, sin-sick soul;
f See the life-stream is flowing,
See the cleansing waves roll,
Step into the current and thou
shalt be whole.

2. *f* 'Tis the voice of that Savior,
Whose merciful call
Freely offers salvation
To one and to all;
He is now beck'ning to Him
Each sin-tainted soul,
And lovingly asking,
"Wilt thou be made whole?"

3. *mf* Are you halting and struggling,
Overpowr'd by your sin,
While the waters are troubled
Can you not enter in?
f Lo, the Savior stands waiting
To strengthen your soul;
He is earnestly pleading,
"Wilt thou be made whole?"

4. *mp* Blessed Savior, assist us
To rest on Thy Word;
Let the soul healing power
On us now be outpoured;
Wash away every sin-spot,
Take perfect control,
Say to each trusting spirit,
"Thy faith makes thee whole."

MFM 2015 SEVENTY DAYS PRAYER & FASTING

PRAISES - TO BE SAID DAILY

Father, in the name of Jesus, I thank You for:

1. Drawing me to prayer and power,
2. The salvation of my soul,
3. Baptizing me with the Holy Spirit,
4. Producing spiritual gifts upon my life,
5. The fruit of the spirit working in me,
6. The wonderful gift of praise,
7. All the ways You have intervened in my affairs,
8. Your divine plan for my life,
9. You will never leave me nor forsake me,
10. Bringing me to a place of maturity and deeper life,
11. Lifting me up when I fall,
12. Keeping me in perfect peace,
13. Making all things work together for good for me,
14. Protecting me from the snares of the fowler and from the noisome pestilence,
15. The wonder-working power in Your Word and in the Blood of the Lamb,
16. Giving Your angels charge over me,
17. Fighting for me against my adversaries,
18. Making me more than a conqueror,
19. Supplying all my needs according to Your riches in glory,
20. Your healing power upon my body, soul and spirit,
21. Flooding my heart with the light of heaven,
22. Always causing me to triumph in Christ Jesus,
23. Turning my curses into blessings,
24. Enabling me to dwell in safety,
25. All the blessings of life,
26. Your greatness, power, glory, majesty, splendor and righteousness,
27. Silencing the foe and the avenger,

28. You are at my right hand and I shall not be moved,
29. You are trustworthy and will help Your own,
30. Not allowing my enemies to rejoice over me,
31. Your wonderful love,
32. You are great and greatly to be praised,
33. Delivering my soul from death and my feet from stumbling,
34. You are my fortress and refuge in time of trouble,
35. Your faithfulness and marvellous deeds,
36. Your act of power and surpassing greatness,
37. Dispersing spiritual blindness from my spirit,
38. Lifting me out of the depths,
39. Preserving me and keeping my feet from slipping,
40. Your name is a strong tower, the righteous runs into it and he is safe.

MFM 2015 SEVENTY DAYS PRAYER & FASTING

PRAYERS FOR CHURCH, MISSIONARY ACTIVITIES AND CHRISTIAN HOMES

TO BE SAID EVERY SUNDAY

1. Thank You, Father, for the promise which says, "I will build my church and the gates of hell shall not prevail against it."
2. I ask for forgiveness of every sin causing disunity and powerlessness in the body of Christ.
3. I take authority over the power of darkness in all its ramifications, in the name of Jesus.
4. I bind and cast out every spirit causing seduction, false doctrine, deception, hypocrisy, pride and error, in Jesus' name.
5. Every plan and strategy of satan against the body of Christ, be bound, in the name of Jesus.
6. Every spirit of prayerlessness, discouragement and vainglory in the body of Christ, be bound, in the name of Jesus.
7. Father, let the spirit of brokenness be released upon us, in Jesus' name.
8. I command the works of the flesh in the lives of the brethren to die, in the name of Jesus.
9. Let the power of the cross and of the Holy Spirit be released to dethrone flesh in our lives, in the name of Jesus.
10. Let the life of our Lord Jesus Christ be truly established in the body of Christ, in the name of Jesus.
11. Every power of selfishness, over-ambition and unteachableness, be broken, in the name of Jesus.
12. Father, grant unto the body of Christ the mind of Christ, forgiving spirit, tolerance, genuine repentance, understanding, submission, humility, brokenness, watchfulness and the mind to commend others better than ourselves, in Jesus' name.
13. I challenge and pull down the forces of disobedience in the lives of the saints, in the name of Jesus.
14. I command these blessings on the body of Christ and ministers

MFM 2015 SEVENTY DAYS PRAYER & FASTING

- love
- longsuffering
- faith
- divine healing
- progress
- prophecy
- the word of knowledge
- divers kinds of tongues
- beauty and glory of God
- dedication and commitment
- joy
- gentleness
- meekness
- divine health
- faith
- discerning of spirits
- the working of miracles
- the interpretation of tongues
- righteousness and holiness
- peace
- goodness
- temperance
- fruitfulness
- the gifts of healing
- the word of wisdom

15. Father, create the thirst and hunger for God and holiness in our lives, in the name of Jesus.
16. O Lord, send down the fire of revival into the body of Christ.
17. O Lord, break and refill Your ministers and vessels afresh.
18. Let there be a full and fresh outpouring of the Holy Ghost upon the ministers of God, in the name of Jesus.
19. O Lord, give unto Your ministers the power for effective prayer life.
20. O Lord, release faithful, committed, dedicated and obedient labourers into the vineyard.
21. I break down the authority and dominion of satan over the souls of men, in the name of Jesus.
22. Every spirit holding the souls of men in captivity, I shatter your back-bone, in the name of Jesus.
23. Every covenant between the souls of men and satan, I dash you to pieces, in the name of Jesus.
24. Let the spirit of steadfastness, consistency, hunger and thirst for the words of God come upon the converts, in Jesus' name.
25. O Lord, release upon all our missionaries and evangelists fresh fire to disgrace territorial spirits.
26. I break the power and the grip of the world upon the souls of men, in the name of Jesus.

MFM 2015 SEVENTY DAYS PRAYER & FASTING

27. I release the spirit of salvation upon areas that have not been reached by the gospel, in the name of Jesus.
28. O Lord, remove all the hindrances to Your purpose for Christian homes.
29. I command the spirit of quarrel, immorality, unfaithfulness, infirmity, disagreement, misunderstanding and intolerance to loose their grips upon Christian homes, in the name of Jesus.
30. Let all Christian homes be a light to the world and a vehicle of salvation, in the name of Jesus.
31. O God, raise up Esther, Ruth and Deborah in this generation, in Jesus' name.
32. Every power destroying joy in the home, be dismantled, in Jesus' name.
33. O Lord, grant us special wisdom to train our children in Your glory.
34. Every Christian marriage that has been re-arranged by the enemy, be corrected, in the name of Jesus.
35. O Lord, let the spirit of wisdom, judgement, submission, gentleness, obedience to God's word and faithfulness in the home, come upon Christian homes.
36. O Lord, remove every wrong spirit from the midst of Your children and put in the right spirit.
37. I take authority, over the plans and activities of satan on ministers' homes, in the name of Jesus.
38. O Lord, increase the power and strength of the ministration of Your words amongst us.
39. Let the kingdom of Christ come into every nation by fire, in Jesus' name.
40. O Lord, dismantle every man-made programme in the body of Christ and set up Your own programme.

MFM 2015 SEVENTY DAYS PRAYER & FASTING

PRAYERS FOR THE NATION
TO BE SAID ON FRIDAYS

SCRIPTURES: 1Tim 2:1-2: I exhort therefore, that, first of all, supplications, prayers, intercessions, and giving of thanks, be made for all men; For kings, and for all that are in authority; that we may lead a quiet and peaceable life in all godliness and honesty.

Jer 1:10: See, I have this day set thee over the nations and over the kingdoms, to root out, and to pull down, and to destroy, and to throw down, to build, and to plant.

Other Scriptures: Isa 61:1-6; Eph 6:10-16.

Praise Worship

1. Father, in the name of Jesus, I confess all the sins and iniquities of the land, of our ancestors, of our leaders, and of the people. E.g., violence, rejection of God, corruption, idolatry, robbery, suspicion, injustice, bitterness, bloody riots, pogroms, rebellion, conspiracy, shedding of innocent blood, tribal conflicts, child-kidnapping and murder, occultism, mismanagement, negligence, etc.
2. I plead for mercy and forgiveness, in the name of Jesus.
3. O Lord, remember our land and redeem it.
4. O Lord, save our land from destruction and judgment.
5. Let Your healing power begin to operate upon our land, in Jesus' name.
6. Let all forces of darkness hindering the move of God in this nation, be rendered impotent, in the name of Jesus.
7. I command the spiritual strongman in charge of this country to be bound and be disgraced, in the name of Jesus.
8. Let every evil establishment and satanic tree in this country be uprooted and cast into fire, in the name of Jesus.
9. I come against every spirit of the anti-Christ working against this nation and I command them to be permanently frustrated, in the name of Jesus.
10. I command the stones of fire from God to fall upon every national satanic operation and activity, in Jesus' name.

MFM 2015 SEVENTY DAYS PRAYER & FASTING

11. Let the desires, plans, devices and expectations of the enemy for this country be completely frustrated, in Jesus' name.
12. Let every satanic curse on this nation fall down to the ground and die, in the name of Jesus.
13. By the blood of Jesus, let all sins, ungodliness, idolatry and vices cease in the land, in the name of Jesus.
14. I break every evil covenant and dedication made upon our land, in the name of Jesus.
15. I plead the blood of Jesus over the nation, in Jesus' name.
16. I decree the will of God for this land, whether the devil likes it or not, in the name of Jesus.
17. Let all contrary powers and authorities in Nigeria be confounded and be put to shame, in the name of Jesus.
18. I close every satanic gate in every city of this country, in Jesus' name.
19. Let every evil throne in this country be dashed to pieces, in Jesus' name.
20. I bind all negative forces operating in the lives of the leaders of this country, in the name of Jesus.
21. O Lord, lay Your hands of fire and power upon all our leaders, in the name of Jesus.
22. I bind every blood-drinking demon in this country, in Jesus' name.
23. Let the Prince of Peace reign in every department of this nation, in the name of Jesus.
24. Let every anti-gospel spirit be frustrated and be rendered impotent, in the name of Jesus.
25. O Lord, give us leaders who will see their roles as a calling, instead of an opportunity to amass wealth.
26. Let all forms of ungodliness be destroyed by the divine fire of burning, in the name of Jesus.
27. O Lord, let our leaders be filled with divine understanding and wisdom.
28. O Lord, let our leaders follow the counsel of God and not of man and demons.
29. O Lord, let our leaders have wisdom and knowledge of God.

MFM 2015 SEVENTY DAYS PRAYER & FASTING

30. O Lord, let our government be the kind that would obtain Your direction and leading.
31. Let every satanic altar in this country receive the fire of God and be burned to ashes, in the name of Jesus.
32. I silence every satanic prophet, priest and practitioner, in the mighty name of Jesus. I forbid them from interfering with the affairs of this nation, in the name of Jesus.
33. Let the blood of Jesus cleanse our land from every blood pollution, in the name of Jesus.
34. I command the fire of God on all idols, sacrifices, rituals, shrines and local satanic thrones in this country, in Jesus' name.
35. I break any conscious and unconscious agreement made between the people of this country and satan, in Jesus' name.
36. I dedicate and claim all our cities for Jesus, in Jesus' name.
37. Let the blessings and presence of the Lord be experienced in all our cities, in the name of Jesus.
38. I decree total paralysis on lawlessness, immorality and drug addiction in this country, in the name of Jesus.
39. Let the power, love and glory of God be established in our land, in the name of Jesus.
40. Let there be thirst and hunger for God in the hearts of Christians of this nation, in the name of Jesus.
41. O Lord, deposit the spirit of revival in Nigeria.
42. O Lord, lay Your hands of power and might upon the Armed Forces and the Police, all government establishments and institutions, all universities and colleges in this country.
43. Let the resurrection power of the Lord Jesus Christ fall upon our economy, in the name of Jesus.
44. Let there be fruitfulness and prosperity in every area of this country, in the name of Jesus.
45. I command every threat to the political, economic and social stability in the land to be paralysed, in the name of Jesus.

MFM 2015 SEVENTY DAYS PRAYER & FASTING

46. I frustrate every satanic external influence over our nation, in Jesus' name.
47. I command confusion and disagreement among the sons of the bondwoman planning to cage the nation, in Jesus' name.
48. I break any covenant between any satanic external influence and our leaders, in the name of Jesus.
49. I paralyse every spirit of wastage of economic resources in this country, in the name of Jesus.
50. Let the spirit of borrowing depart completely from this country, in the name of Jesus.
51. O Lord, show Yourself mighty in the affairs of this nation.
52. Let the Kingdom of Christ come into this nation, in Jesus' name.
53. O Lord, do new things in our country to show Your power and greatness to the heathen.
54. Let the Kingdom of our Lord Jesus Christ come into the heart of every person in this country, in the name of Jesus.
55. O Lord, have mercy upon this nation.
56. Let all the glory of this nation that has departed be restored, in Jesus' name.
57. Let all un-evangelized areas of this country be reached with the Gospel of our Lord Jesus Christ, in the name of Jesus.
58. O Lord, send forth labourers into Your vineyard to reach the unreached in this country.
59. I dismantle the stronghold of poverty in this nation, in the name of Jesus.
60. O Lord, install Your agenda for this nation.
61. Let every power of darkness operating in our educational institutions be disgraced, in the name of Jesus.
62. Let the satanic representatives of key posts in this country be dismantled, in the name of Jesus.
63. Let every evil spiritual throne behind all physical thrones in Nigeria be dismantled, in the name of Jesus.
64. Let every satanic covenant made on behalf of this country by anyone be nullified, in the name of Jesus.

MFM 2015 SEVENTY DAYS PRAYER & FASTING

65. I trample upon the serpents and scorpions, of ethnic clashes in this country, in the name of Jesus.
66. I decree a realignment of the situation around Christians, to favour them in this country, in the name of Jesus.
67. I dethrone every strange king installed in the spirit over this country, in the name of Jesus.
68. Let all principalities, powers, rulers of darkness and spiritual wickedness in heavenly places militating against this nation be bound and disgraced, in the name of Jesus.
69. Let righteousness reign in every part of this nation, in Jesus' name.
70. Praises.

MFM 2015 SEVENTY DAYS PRAYER & FASTING

SECTION 1 - PROMPTING TO PRAISE

Scripture Reading: Psalm 118

Confession: Psalms 107:15-16: Oh that men would praise the Lord for his goodness, and for his wonderful works to the children of men! For he hath broken the gates of brass, and cut the bars of iron in sunder.

SECTION I DAY I (03-08-2015)

Reading through the Bible in 70 Days (Day 1 - Genesis 1:1 - 18:20)
Devotional Songs (Pages 11-14)
Praise Worship
Prayer of Praise and Thanksgiving (Pages 15 & 16)

1. O God, I thank You, for You have gloriously triumphed (Ex.15:1)
2. O God, my Father I thank You, for throwing my enemies with their horses into the sea. (Ex. 15:2).
3. O God, I thank You, for You are my strength, my song and for You becoming my salvation.(Ex.15:2).
4. O God, I thank You, for You are my God and the God of Abraham, Isaac and Jacob; I praise and exalt You. (Ex.15:2)
5. O God, I thank You, for You are highly exalted.(Ex.15:21)
6. O God, I thank You, for You rescued me from the hand of my enemies.(Ex.18:10)
7. O God, I thank You, for Your greatness, because You are the rock; all Your ways are perfect and are just.(Deut. 32:3).
8. O God, I thank You, for You do no wrong; You are upright and just. (Deut. 32:4b).
9. O God, I thank You, for lifting my horn (strength) high.(1 Sam.2:10).
10. O God, I thank You, for taking Your rightful place in my life.(2 Sam.6:14).

MFM 2015 SEVENTY DAYS PRAYER & FASTING

11. O God, I thank You, for You are worthy of praise and for saving me from my enemies.(2 Sam 22:4).
12. O God, I thank You, for You avenge me and put nations under me; thank You also, exalting me above my foes and rescuing me from violent men.(2 Sam 22:49)
13. O God, I thank You, for You have delighted in me and had lifted me up .(1 Kings 10:9).
14. O God, I thank You, for Your wonderful acts and Your holy name (1 Chronicles 16:9).
15. O God, I thank You, for You are great and worthy of praise (1 Chronicles 16:26).
16. O God, I thank You, for Your mercy endures forever.(1 Chronicles 16:41).
17. O God, I thank You, for Your hands have strength and power, to exalt and give strength.
18. Father, we thank You, for we have a song to sing for Your creative power, that brought all things to be, in the name of Jesus.
19. Father, we thank You, for we have a song to sing for Your sustaining grace, that has touched us and held us, in the name of Jesus.
20. Father, we thank You, for Your sustaining grace that has fed us and guided us in each step of the way, in the name of Jesus.
21. Father, we praise You, for a Saviour who lived our lives, walked our earth and died in our place, in the name of Jesus.

SECTION I DAY 2 (04-08-2015)

Confession: **Psalms 107:15-16:** Oh that men would praise the Lord for his goodness, and for his wonderful works to the children of men! For he hath broken the gates of brass, and cut the bars of iron in sunder.

Reading through the Bible in 70 Days (Day 2 - Genesis 18:21 - 31:16)

Devotional Songs (Pages 11-14)

MFM 2015 SEVENTY DAYS PRAYER & FASTING

Praise Worship

Prayer of Praise and Thanksgiving (Pages 15 & 16)

22. Father, we praise You, for the Holy Spirit who empowers us for worship and enables us to sing our song of praise, in the name of Jesus.
23. Father, we praise You, for in Christ, all our end becomes His new beginning and all our weaknesses, are clothed in His strength, in the name of Jesus.
24. Father, we praise You, for in Christ our times of emptiness are filled with hope, in the name of Jesus.
25. O God, I thank You, for You made the heavens and the earth. (2 Chronicles 2:12).
26. O God, I thank You, for Your enduring mercy. (2 Chronicles 7:3,6, 20:21).
27. O God, I thank You, for the splendour of Your holiness. (2 Chronicles 20:21).
28. O God, I thank You, because You gave me great joy (Neh. 12:43).
29. O God, I thank You, because You give and take away (Job 1:21).
30. O God, I thank You, because of Your righteousness (Ps. 7:17).
31. O God, I thank You, because You silence the enemies, the foes and the avenger (Ps 8:2).
32. O God, I thank You, because You are enthroned in Zion (Ps 9:11).
33. O God, I thank You, because You have been so good to me (Ps 13:16).
34. O God, I thank You, because You counsel Your own (Ps 16:7).
35. O God, I thank You, because You are worthy of praise (Ps 18:3).
36. O God, I thank You, because You avenge and subdue the nations. (Ps 18:47).
37. O God, I thank You, because You give great victories (Ps 18:50).
38. O God, I thank You, because You had heard our cry for mercy (Ps 28:16).
39. O God, I thank You, because You show great everlasting kindness to me and my descendants (Ps 18:50).
40. O God, I thank You, because You are my strength and my shield (Ps 28:7).

41. O God, I thank You, because You are trustworthy and You help Your own (Ps 28:7).
42. O God, I thank You, for You are my strength and a fortress of salvation for Your anointed (Ps 28:8).

SECTION I DAY 3 (05-08-2015)

Confession: Psalms 107:15-16: Oh that men would praise the Lord for his goodness, and for his wonderful works to the children of men! For he hath broken the gates of brass, and cut the bars of iron in sunder.

Reading through the Bible in 70 Days (Day 3 - Genesis 31:17 - 44:10)

Devotional Songs (Pages 11-14)

Praise Worship

Prayer of Praise and Thanksgiving (Pages 15 & 16)

43. O God, I thank You for disallowing evil testimonies over my life and my family.
44. O God, I thank You, for empowering me to defeat the Goliath of my life.
45. O God, I thank You, for putting my enemies under my feet.
46. O God, I thank You, for making every satanic plan against my life to fail woefully.
47. O God, I thank You, for the heavenly salt that sweetens my Marah.
48. O God, I thank You, for breaking to pieces the gates of brass and cutting the bars of iron erected against my life.
49. O God, I thank You, for making every evil arrow fired at my life to back fire.
50. O God, I thank You, for disengaging the satanic network fashioned against my life, in the second heaven and on the earth.
51. O God, I thank You, for making my Haman to die in my place.
52. O God, I thank You, for Your eyes that neither sleep nor slumber, that watch over me day and night.

53. O God, I thank You, for guiding me by Your pillar of cloud in the day and fire by the night.
54. O God, I thank You, for overturning the table of my enemies in every aspect of my life.
55. O God, I thank You, for disorganizing and confusing the language of my enemies.
56. O God, I thank You, for prospering the land of my life and for the heavenly fertilizer that has made me fruitful.
57. O God, I thank You, for the living water that has quenched my thirst for sins.
58. O God, I thank You, for destroying every satanic hijacker that has been assigned against my life in the spiritual and in the physical realms.
59. O God, I thank You, for terminating every satanic appointment and schedule that is against my progress in life.
60. O God, I thank You, for terminating every terminal problem that is working against my success and achievement in life.
61. O God, I thank You, for making it impossible for generational problems and curses to prosper in my life and family.
62. O God, I thank You, for disallowing Satan to share Your glory in my life.
63. O God, I thank You, for uprooting and destroying every root of poverty in my life and planting the tree of prosperity instead.

SECTION I DAY 4 (06-08-2015)

Confession: Psalms 107:15-16: Oh that men would praise the Lord for his goodness, and for his wonderful works to the children of men! For he hath broken the gates of brass, and cut the bars of iron in sunder.

Reading through the Bible in 70 Days (Day 4 - Genesis 44:11 - 50:26; Exodus 1:1 - 10:2)

Devotional Songs (Pages 11-14)

MFM 2015 SEVENTY DAYS PRAYER & FASTING

Praise Worship
Prayer of Praise and Thanksgiving (Pages 15 & 16)

64. O God, I thank You, for making me god over every Pharaoh of my life as You did for Joseph in the land of Egypt.
65. O God, I thank You, for sending every enchantment and divination of the enemy back to them.
66. O God, I thank You, for breaking the curse of limitation and stagnation upon my life.
67. O God, I thank You, for breaking the backbone of every household enemy, that has vowed over his dead body against my prosperity and advancement in life.
68. O God, I thank You, for not allowing my vehicle of life to sink in the deep waters.
69. O God, I thank You, for Your mighty hands that have rescued me from the lion's den, which the enemy has prepared for my destruction.
70. O God, I thank You, for leading me through the wilderness of downfall and for defeating every satanic expectation that is against my life.
71. Lord, we praise You, for our brokenness has found the only source of peace and wholeness.
72. Lord, we praise You, for in Christ the joy of heaven burst into our days and hours.
73. Lord, we praise You, for by Your Holy Spirit all the things of earth find their centre and purpose in Him.
74. Lord, we praise You, for in Christ our lives receive a purpose deep and wide.
75. Father, we praise You, for Jesus Christ who gave Himself as a living sacrifice.
76. Lord, we praise You, for You have called us to be Your faithful people.
77. Lord, we praise You, for in Christ You have given us hope.
78. Lord, we praise You, for in Christ You have given us peace.
79. Lord, we praise You, for You have given us a new purpose.

80. Lord, we praise You, for the gifts which You flood our lives with.
81. Lord, we praise You, for the gift of laughter that brightens our darkest day.
82. Lord, we praise You, for the grace of the Lord Jesus Christ and Your love.
83. Father, we thank You, for the mercy You have displayed, in Jesus' name.
84. Father, we thank You, for the forgiveness You have offered, in Jesus' name.

SECTION I DAY 5 (07-08-2015)

Confession: Psalms 107:15-16: Oh that men would praise the Lord for his goodness, and for his wonderful works to the children of men! For he hath broken the gates of brass, and cut the bars of iron in sunder.

Reading through the Bible in 70 Days (Day 5 - Exodus 10:3 - 25:29)
Devotional Songs (Pages 11-14)
Praise Worship
Prayer of Praise and Thanksgiving (Pages 15 & 16)

85. Father, we thank You, for the renewal You have brought, in Jesus' name.
86. Father, we thank You, for all You are, all You have been, and all You shall continue to be, in the name of Jesus.
87. Father, we thank You, for the ways You have guided and taught us, in the name of Jesus.
88. Father, we thank You, for the times You have offered us strength and support, in the name of Jesus.
89. Father, we thank You, for the fellowship we have shared, in Jesus' name.
90. Father, we thank You, for the encouragement we were given and received, in the name of Jesus.
91. Father, we thank You, for the successes we have achieved, in Jesus' name.
92. Father, we thank You, for the dreams we still have, in Jesus' name.

93. Gracious God, we thank You, because we owe our very lives to You, in the name of Jesus.
94. Gracious God, we thank You, because You have watched over us from our birth, in the name of Jesus.
95. Gracious God, we thank You, for tenderly nurturing us and showering us with love, in the name of Jesus.
96. Gracious God, we thank You, because You have given us strength in times of need, in the name of Jesus.
97. Gracious God, we thank You, because You comfort us in times of distress, in the name of Jesus.
98. Gracious God, we thank You, for Your encouragement in times of despair, in the name of Jesus.
99. Gracious God, we thank You, for Your guidance in times of uncertainty, in the name of Jesus.
100. Gracious God, we thank You, because whatever we face You have been with us, in the name of Jesus.
101. Father, we thank You, for loving us with an unquenchable love, in the name of Jesus.
102. Father, we thank You, for when we sing Your praise, You reveal Yourself as the One who is worthy of all our adoration, in the name of Jesus.
103. Father, we thank You, for You point us to Christ and His sacrifice for our sins, in the name of Jesus.
104. Father, we thank You, for You have shown us in Jesus that everything is safe in Your hands, in the name of Jesus.
105. Father, we thank You, for nothing we give back to You will ever be wasted, in the name of Jesus.

MFM 2015 SEVENTY DAYS PRAYER & FASTING

SECTION I DAY 6 (08-08-2015)

Confession: Psalms 107:15-16: Oh that men would praise the Lord for his goodness, and for his wonderful works to the children of men! For he hath broken the gates of brass, and cut the bars of iron in sunder.

Reading through the Bible in 70 Days (Day 6 - Exodus 25:30 - 39:5)

Devotional Songs (Pages 11-14)

Praise Worship

Prayer of Praise and Thanksgiving (Pages 15 & 16)

106. Father, we thank You, for Your love is the ultimate answer to everything we face, in the name of Jesus.
107. Father, we thank You, for You have demonstrated in Christ's life and death, that as You had the first word so Your word in Christ will always be Your final word, in the name of Jesus.
108. Father, we praise You, for You are able to see us through, in Jesus' name.
109. Father, we praise You, for You are able to give us strength, in Jesus' name.
110. Father, we praise You, for You are able to bless us beyond words, in the name of Jesus.
111. Father, we praise You, for You are able to do more than we can ever ask or think of, in the name of Jesus.
112. Father, we thank You, because You are unsearchable and inexhaustible, in the name of Jesus.
113. Father, we thank You, for You have called us to be Your children, in the name of Jesus.
114. Father, we thank You, for You love us passionately, fiercely, devotedly and wholeheartedly, in the name of Jesus.
115. Father, we thank You, for You are always there when we need You, in the name of Jesus.

116. Father, we praise You, because everything You do is right and all Your ways are just and those who walk in pride, You are able to humble, in the name of Jesus.
117. We praise You, for You have done great things for us, holy is Your name, in the name of Jesus.
118. Father, we praise You, because Your mercy extends to those who fear You, from generation to generation, in the name of Jesus.
119. We thank You, Father, for You have performed mighty deeds with Your arms; You scattered those who were proud in their innermost thoughts, in the name of Jesus.
120. We give You praise, Father, because You have brought down wicked rulers from their thrones but lifted up the humble, in the name of Jesus.
121. We thank You, Father, because You fill the hungry with good things but send the rich away empty, in the name of Jesus.
122. Father, we praise You, for You are the Father of compassion and God of all comforts, who comforts us so that we may comfort others, in Jesus' name.
123. Thank You, Father, for blessing us with all spiritual blessings in heavenly places in Christ, in the name of Jesus.
124. Father, we praise You, for You are Holy, Almighty, and Eternal, in the name of Jesus.
125. Father, You are worthy to receive glory, honour and power, in Jesus' name.
126. Thank You, Father, for You created all things, and for Your pleasure they were created, in the name of Jesus.

SECTION I DAY 7 (09-08-2015)

Confession: Psalms 107:15-16: Oh that men would praise the Lord for his goodness, and for his wonderful works to the children of men! For he hath broken the gates of brass, and cut the bars of iron in sunder.

MFM 2015 SEVENTY DAYS PRAYER & FASTING

Reading through the Bible in 70 Days (Day 7 - Exod 39:6 - 40:38; Lev 1:1-14:3)
Devotional Songs (Pages 11-14)
Praise Worship
Prayer of Praise and Thanksgiving (Pages 15 & 16)

127. Thank You, Jesus, for You are worthy to receive power, wealth, wisdom, strength, glory, honour and praise, in the name of Jesus.
128. We thank You, Father, for You alone are holy; all nations will come and worship You, and Your righteous acts have been revealed, in Jesus' name.
129. Father, we praise You, because salvation, glory and power belong to You, in the name of Jesus.
130. Father, we thank You, for the Lord God Almighty reigns, in Jesus' name.
131. Father, we thank You, for You are our Healer and Restorer, in Jesus' name.
132. Father, we thank You, because You are our Banner, in Jesus' name.
133. Father, we thank You, for Your exalted Headship, in Jesus' name.
134. Father, we thank You, for You are a Consuming Fire, in Jesus' name.
135. Father, we thank You, for the occasions You have specially surrounded us with Your love and compassion, in the name of Jesus.
136. Father, we praise You, Lord, who through Your life, death and resurrection offered us freedom that cannot be paid for in any other way.
137. We will declare Your name to the brethren; in the congregation of the righteous we will praise You, in the name of Jesus.
138. We praise You, Father, for we fear the Lord, in the name of Jesus.
139. Praise be to the Lord, for He has heard our cry for mercy, in Jesus' name.
140. Father, our heart leaps for joy and we will give thanks to You in songs, in the name of Jesus.
141. We ascribe to the Lord, the glory due His name, in the name of Jesus.
142. We rejoice and sing to the Lord, for He has done great things for us, in the name of Jesus.

143. We sing joyfully to the Lord, because it is fitting for the upright to praise him, in the name of Jesus.
144. Father, we praise You with all our being; we sing to You a new song, in the name of Jesus.
145. Praise the Lord with the harp; make music to him on the ten-stringed lyre. Sing to him a new song; play skilfully and shout for joy.
146. I will extol the Lord at all times; His praise will always be on my lips.
147. My soul will boast in the Lord; let the afflicted hear and rejoice. Glorify the Lord with me; let us exalt his name together.

SECTION I DAY 8 (10-08-2015)

Confession: Psalms 107:15-16: Oh that men would praise the Lord for his goodness, and for his wonderful works to the children of men! For he hath broken the gates of brass, and cut the bars of iron in sunder.

Reading through the Bible in 70 Days (Day 8 - Leviticus 14:4 - 26:35)

Devotional Songs (Pages 11-14)

Praise Worship

Prayer of Praise and Thanksgiving (Pages 15 & 16)

148. I will give You thanks in the great assembly; among throngs of people I will praise You.
149. My tongue will speak of Your righteousness and of Your praises all day long.
150. He put a new song in my mouth, a hymn of praise to our God. Many will see and fear and put their trust in the Lord.
151. Praise be to the Lord, the God of Israel, from everlasting to everlasting. Amen and Amen.
152. In God we will make our boast all day long, and we will praise Your name forever.

153. I will perpetuate Your memory through all generations; therefore the nations will praise You for ever and ever.
154. Clap your hands, all you nations; shout unto God with cries of joy.
155. How awesome is the Lord Most High, the great King over all the earth.
156. Great is the Lord and most worthy of praise, in the city of our God, in his holy mountain.
157. I will praise You forever for what You have done; in Your name I will hope, for Your name is good.
158. I will praise You in the presence of Your saints.
159. Father, we thank You, for enriching our journey with Your presence and power.
160. O God, I thank You,, for You are the Lord of lords.
161. O God, I thank You,, for You settle the barren woman in her home as a happy mother of children.
162. Heavenly Father, I thank You, for You are the Morning Star.
163. O God, I thank You,, for all Your commands are righteous.
164. O God, I thank You,, for You are Jehovah-M'kadesh, my Sanctifier.
165. O God, I thank You,, for You commanded and everything was created.
166. O God, I thank You,, for You are Jehovah-Rohi, my Shepherd.
167. O God, I thank You,, for Your Acts of Great Power.
168. O God, I thank You,, for You are the Resurrection and the Life.

SECTION I DAY 9 (11-08-2015)

Confession: Psalms 107:15-16: Oh that men would praise the Lord for his goodness, and for his wonderful works to the children of men! For he hath broken the gates of brass, and cut the bars of iron in sunder.

MFM 2015 SEVENTY DAYS PRAYER & FASTING

Reading through the Bible in 70 Days (Day 9-Leviticus 26:36 - 27:34; Numbers 1:1 - 10:16)

Devotional Songs (Pages 11-14)

Praise Worship

Prayer of Praise and Thanksgiving (Pages 15 & 16)

169. O God, I thank You,, for You give wisdom to the wise and knowledge to the discerning.
170. My Father and my God, I thank You, for You are the Way, the Truth and the Life.
171. My Father and my God, I thank You, for You reveal the deep and hidden things; You know what lies in darkness.
172. Father, we thank You, and praise You, for the value You see in all Your creatures, in the name of Jesus.
173. Father, we thank You, for Your grace that has lit the spark of faith within us, in the name of Jesus.
174. Lord, we thank You, for Your unseen hand upon our lives.
175. Lord, we thank You, for Your endless love on which we can depend now and for all eternity.
176. Father, we thank You, for the harvest of love that we have received through the life, death and resurrection of Jesus Christ, in Jesus' name.
177. Father, we thank You, for when we take a step of faith You prove to be worthy of our trust, in the name of Jesus.
178. Great Father of Glory, I thank You, because on Your hands are the depths of the earth, and the Mountain peaks belong to You.
179. O God, I thank You, for the marvellous things You have done.
180. O God, I thank You, for redeeming my life from the pit and crowning me with compassion and love.
181. O Lord, I thank you for being the Strength of my soul.

182. O God, I thank You, for You are the God of Justice.
183. O God, I thank You, for Your kingdom is an eternal kingdom and Your dominion endures from to generation.
184. O God, I thank You, for You are the God of Patience.
185. O God, I thank You, for You are the God of the Holy Prophets.
186. I praise You Lord, for the name of Jesus is able to destroy nations.
187. I give You all glory Lord, for the name of Jesus is able to bring signs and wonders.
188. I exalt You Lord, for You are with us when we gather together in the name of Jesus.
189. O God, I thank You, for the name of Jesus gives me power over demons.

SECTION I DAY 10 (12-08-2015)

Confession: Psalms 107:15-16: Oh that men would praise the Lord for his goodness, and for his wonderful works to the children of men! For he hath broken the gates of brass, and cut the bars of iron in sunder.

Reading through the Bible in 70 Days (Day 10 - Numbers 10:17 - 24:3)

Devotional Songs (Pages 11-14)

Praise Worship

Prayer of Praise and Thanksgiving (Pages 15 & 16)

190. O God, I thank You, for in the name of Jesus I can confront my enemies.
191. O God, I thank You, for at the name of Jesus every knee will bow.
192. O God, I thank You, for the name of Jesus will be written on my forehead.
193. O God, I thank You, for You are the Omnipresent One.
194. O God, I thank You, for You are the Omniscient One.
195. Great Father, I thank You, for You are the Unchangeable One.

196. Good Lord, I thank You, for You are before the foundations of the earth

MFM 2015 SEVENTY DAYS PRAYER & FASTING

197. O Lord, we praise You, for You are ever at work in our lives and our world.
198. Thank You, Lord because You are greater than our minds can grasp.
199. Thank You, Lord because You are higher than our highest thoughts.
200. We praise You, for You are the source of all that is and has been.
201. Thank You, Lord, because You are at work in our world and in our lives.
202. Lord of all ages, we thank You for the days and the years of our lives.
203. Lord, we thank You,, because You always receive us with open arms and love that never ends.
204. Lord of all ages, we thank You for Your patience that has come with the years.
205. Lord of all ages, we thank You for Your greatness, Your glory and Your power.
206. Lord of all ages, we thank You for Your ageless love and Your endless patience with Your wayward children.
207. Lord of all ages, we thank You for Christ who was crucified without reaching old age.
208. Father, we bless You, for You are from everlasting to everlasting, in the name of Jesus.
209. Blessed be Your glorious name, Father, and may it be exalted above all blessing and praise, in the name of Jesus.
210. Father, we praise You, for You are exalted in Your power, in Jesus' name.

SECTION CONFESSIONS

No counsel of the wicked, shall stand against me, in the name of Jesus. Unto me, shall God do exceedingly abundantly above all that I ask, seek, desire and think, according to the power that He had made to work in me, in the name of Jesus. As it is written, I shall be a crown of glory in the hand of God, a royal diadem in the hand of my Maker. I begin to shine as a shining light. The light of God is in me. The word of God, has made me a brazen wall, a fortified city, an iron pillar. My presence terrifies the enemy. He trembles, feels much pain and travails at the sound of my voice which the Lord has empowered. For it is written, wherever the voice of the king is, there is authority. My appearance, is as the appearance of a horse. So, I leap, I run like mighty men. When I fall upon the sword, it cannot hurt me, in the name of Jesus.

It is written, "If God be for us, who can be against us?" God is with me; I have no reason to fear, in the name of Jesus. I receive the ammunition of angelic guidance and operations in my life right now, in the name of Jesus. The angels have been ordered by God to take charge of me in all my ways and I receive them, they go ahead of me wherever I go and in whatever I do; they go forth and make all the crooked ways straight from me, in the name of Jesus. The angels of God watch over me in the day time and in the night time. They make sure that no evil whatsoever befalls me, in Jesus' name. I send the angels of God to pursue all my enemies and make them like chaff in the wind, in the name of Jesus. I also send a grievous whirlwind to hit them, to destroy them and cast them into the bottomless pit, in the name of Jesus.

SECTION VIGIL
(To be done at night between the hours of 12 midnight and 2am)
HYMN FOR THE VIGIL (Page 14)

1. O Lord, give unto me the Spirit of revelation and wisdom in the knowledge of Yourself.
2. O Lord, make Your way plain before my face on this issue.
3. O Lord, reveal to me every secret behind any problem that I have.
4. O Lord, bring to light everything planned against me in darkness.
5. I remove my name, from the book of those who grope and stumble in darkness, in the name of Jesus.
6. O Lord, make me a vessel capable of knowing Your secret things.

MFM 2015 SEVENTY DAYS PRAYER & FASTING

7. O Lord, let the teeth of the enemy, over our nation break, in Jesus' name.
8. I cast out, my pursuers, as the dirt in the street, in Jesus' name.
9. By Your favour, O Lord, the people whom I have not known shall serve me, in the name of Jesus.
10. As soon as they hear of me, they shall obey me, the strangers shall submit themselves unto me, in the name of Jesus.
11. You dark strangers in my life, fade away and be afraid out of their close places, in the name of Jesus.
12. O God, avenge me and subdue my adversaries under me, in Jesus' name.
13. O Lord, hear me in the day of trouble, and let the name of the God of Jacob defend me, in the name of Jesus.
14. O Lord, send me help from Your sanctuary and strengthen me out of Zion, in the name of Jesus.
15. O Lord, hear my voice whenever I call, in the name of Jesus.
16. O God, visit every power lying against me with destruction, in Jesus' name.
17. O Lord, let the dry wind from heaven blow down the pillars of their confident buildings, in the name of Jesus.
18. Hot coals of fire from heaven, blow down their houses, in Jesus' name.
19. O Lord, let the enemies of this country, become merely another story told, in the name of Jesus.
20. My Father, let my enemies fall, by their own counsel, in Jesus' name.
21. O Lord, cast out my enemies in the multitude of their transgressions, in Jesus' name.

MFM 2015 SEVENTY DAYS PRAYER & FASTING

SECTION 2 - ENGAGING YOUR PERSONAL PENTECOST

Scripture Reading: Acts 1

Confession: Acts 2:17 And it shall come to pass in the last days, saith God, I will pour out of my Spirit upon all flesh: and your sons and your daughters shall prophesy, and your young men shall see visions, and your old men shall dream dreams:

SECTION 2 DAY 1 (13-08-2015)

Reading through the Bible in 70 Days (Day 11 - Numbers 24:4 - 36:13; Deuteronomy 1:1 - 1:2)

Devotional Songs (Pages 11-14)

Praise Worship

Prayer of Praise and Thanksgiving (Pages 14 & 15)

1. Holy Ghost fire, incubate my body, soul and spirit for complete deliverance, in the name of Jesus.
2. Holy Ghost fire, purge my body, soul and spirit for complete deliverance, in the name of Jesus.
3. Holy Ghost fire, laminate my life for complete protection, in the name of Jesus.
4. Holy Ghost fire, convert me to God's weapon of war, in the name of Jesus.
5. I receive power, to terrify every spiritual terrorist, in the name of Jesus.
6. My Father, my Father, my Father, give me fresh fire to fight, in Jesus' name.
7. Anointing that terrifies the enemy, come upon me, in the name of Jesus.
8. Anointing of the overcomer, come upon me, in the name of Jesus.
9. Power of the Most High, overshadow and incubate my life, in Jesus' name.
10. Fire power, that cannot be resisted or insulted, fall upon me, in Jesus' name.
11. Every agenda of wasters, every agenda of emptiers, assigned to embarrass me, scatter, in the name of Jesus.

MFM 2015 SEVENTY DAYS PRAYER & FASTING

12. The fire that fell at Pentecost, overshadow me now, in the name of Jesus.
13. Powers assigned to make me a negative example, scatter and die, in the name of Jesus.
14. Powers drinking the blood of my anointing, die, in the name of Jesus.
15. Anti ministerial chain of my father's house, break, in the name of Jesus.
16. Powers gathered to cut off the wings of my eagles, scatter unto desolation, in the name of Jesus.
17. Disgrace producers, I am not your victim, die, in the name of Jesus.
18. Voices from my foundation, contesting with my calling, die by fire, in the name of Jesus.
19. My Father, cover my defenceless head, in the name of Jesus.
20. Power to meet the needs of my generation, fall upon me, in the name of Jesus.
21. Anti ministerial attitudes, characters and habits in my life, die by fire, in the name of Jesus.

SECTION 2 DAY 2 (14-08-2015)

Confession: Acts 2:17 And it shall come to pass in the last days, saith God, I will pour out of my Spirit upon all flesh: and your sons and your daughters shall prophesy, and your young men shall see visions, and your old men shall dream dreams:

Reading through the Bible in 70 Days (Day 12 - Deuteronomy 1:3 - 15:20)
Devotional Songs (Pages 11-14)
Praise Worship
Prayer of Praise and Thanksgiving (Pages 15 & 16)

22. Every trap of Jezebel, set for me, break, in the name of Jesus.
23. Holy Ghost, laminate my life, in the name of Jesus.
24. Blood of Jesus, laminate my life, in the name of Jesus.

MFM 2015 SEVENTY DAYS PRAYER & FASTING

25. Holy thirst and hunger for the things of God, fall upon me, in the name of Jesus.
26. Power that cannot be reproached, come upon me, in the name of Jesus.
27. Power that cannot be insulted, come upon me now, in the name of Jesus.
28. O God, arise and bombard me with spiritual gifts, in the name of Jesus.
29. Thou power of spiritual carelessness, die by fire, in the name of Jesus.
30. Power of the Most High, overshadow my life, in the name of Jesus.
31. Holy Ghost, advertise Your power in my life, in the name of Jesus.
32. My Father, arise in Your fury, silence my silencers, in the name of Jesus.
33. Rages and sieges against my calling, expire, in the name of Jesus.
34. O Lord, let me be wiser than my enemies, in the name of Jesus.
35. My Father, give me the eyes of Elisha and the ears of Samuel, in Jesus' name.
36. Ministerial scandals, run away from my calling, in the name of Jesus.
37. I reject, ministerial embarrassment, by the power in the blood of Jesus, in the name of Jesus.
38. Opportunity wasters, die by fire, in the name of Jesus.
39. Lord, ignite in me an unquenchable passion for growth, in the name of Jesus.
40. Goliath, Herod and Sanbalat forces harassing my calling, die by fire, in the name of Jesus.
41. I go, from strength to strength and from glory to glory, by the power in the blood of Jesus, in the name of Jesus.
42. I bind, ministerial stagnancy with the fetters of iron and cast them into the fire, in the name of Jesus.

MFM 2015 SEVENTY DAYS PRAYER & FASTING

SECTION 2 DAY 3 (15-08-2015)

Confession: Acts 2:17 And it shall come to pass in the last days, saith God, I will pour out of my Spirit upon all flesh: and your sons and your daughters shall prophesy, and your young men shall see visions, and your old men shall dream dreams:

Reading through the Bible in 70 Days (Day 13 - Deut. 15:21- 32:26)
Devotional Songs (Pages 11-14)
Praise Worship
Prayer of Praise and Thanksgiving (Pages 15 & 16)

43. Every agenda of the wasters for my calling, I bury you now, in Jesus' name.
44. Holy Ghost, fulfil Your purpose in me now, in the name of Jesus
45. Holy Ghost, fill me that I might bring forth good fruit, in the name of Jesus.
46. Holy Ghost fire, begin to arrest the spirit of fear in every department of my life, in the name of Jesus.
47. Holy Ghost fire, begin to arrest the spirit of doubt in every department of my life, in the name of Jesus.
48. Holy Ghost fire, begin to arrest the spirit of deceit in every department of my life, in the name of Jesus.
49. Holy Ghost fire, begin to arrest the spirit of unbelief in every department of my life, in the name of Jesus.
50. Holy Ghost fire, begin to arrest the spirit of strife in every department of my life, in the name of Jesus.
51. Holy Ghost fire, begin to arrest unforgiving spirit in every department of my life, in the name of Jesus.
52. Holy Ghost, overshadow my life, in the name of Jesus.
53. Fire of God, arise for my sake, sanitize my life, in the name of Jesus.
54. Holy Ghost, fill me from the top of my head to the soles of my feet, in the name of Jesus.

55. Power, that cannot be ridiculed or mocked, come upon me, in Jesus' name.
56. Power, to pursue my pursuers, fall upon me now, in the name of Jesus.
57. Holy Ghost fire, baptise me afresh, in the name of Jesus.
58. My Father, lay Your hands upon my life and let my life advertise Your power, in the name of Jesus.
59. Anointing to silence my silencers, come upon me now, in the name of Jesus.
60. Anointing to torment my tormentors, fall upon me now, in the name of Jesus.
61. Anointing to pursuer my pursuers, fall upon me now, in the name of Jesus.
62. My name, become hot coals of fire in the covens of darkness, in Jesus' name.
63. You words of my mouth, carry fire that the enemy cannot resist, in the name of Jesus.

SECTION 2 DAY 4 (16-08-2015)

Confession: Acts 2:17 And it shall come to pass in the last days, saith God, I will pour out of my Spirit upon all flesh: and your sons and your daughters shall prophesy, and your young men shall see visions, and your old men shall dream dreams:

Reading through the Bible in 70 Days (Day 14 -Deuteronomy 32:27 - 34:12; Joshua 1:1 - 15:27)

Devotional Songs (Pages 11-14)

Praise Worship

Prayer of Praise and Thanksgiving (Pages 15 & 16)

64. Holy Ghost and fire, fill my body, soul and spirit, in the name of Jesus.
65. Lay Your hands upon me, O Lord, by Your fire, in the name of Jesus.
66. Every rope tying me down to the same spot spiritually, catch fire now, in the name of Jesus.

67. Every agenda of sluggishness, introduced into my destiny, catch fire, in the name of Jesus.
68. Father, let my hypocrisy, die, in the name of Jesus.
69. I repent, of any contribution I have made to advance any unrighteousness, in the name of Jesus.
70. Father, help me to save my own life, in the name of Jesus.
71. Every mountain, that is boasting against me, who art thou, the Lord rebukes you, in the name of Jesus.
72. Everywhere I enter, my God is there and He will answer by fire, in Jesus' name.
73. Mountain of frustration, get out of my situations, in the name of Jesus.
74. By fire, by force, I break every satanic strangulation upon my life, in the name of Jesus.
75. I decree by the decree of heaven, that I am not of those that go back to perdition, in the name of Jesus.
76. My Father, my Father, my Father, let Your glory possess me, in Jesus' name.
77. Every spiritual irritation upon my life, lift away, in the name of Jesus.
78. Every spiritual limitation upon my life, lift away, in the name of Jesus.
79. Father, let Your fire destroy every evil thing in my flesh, in the name of Jesus.
80. Father, heal me of any form of evil conscience, in the name of Jesus.
81. Father, sprinkle my heart with the blood of Jesus.
82. Father, choose me for signs and wonders, in the name of Jesus.
83. I stand against, every power of defilement, in the name of Jesus.
84. Every power of defilement defiling my life, die, in the name of Jesus.

SECTION 2 DAY 5 (17-08-2015)

Confession: Acts 2:17 And it shall come to pass in the last days, saith God, I will pour out of my Spirit upon all flesh: and your sons and your daughters shall prophesy, and your young men shall see visions, and your old men shall dream dreams:

Reading through the Bible in 70 Days (Day 15 -Joshua 15:28 - 24:33; Judges 1:1 - 6:20 Day 14 -Deuteronomy 32:27 - 34:12; Joshua 1:1 - 15:27)

Devotional Songs (Pages 11-14)

Praise Worship

Prayer of Praise and Thanksgiving (Pages 15 & 16)

85. Holy Ghost fire, destroy every defilement in my body, in the name of Jesus.
86. Every agent of defilement in my life, I shake you off, in the name of Jesus.
87. I fire back, every arrow of defilement by the power in the blood of Jesus, in the name of Jesus.
88. Every power, assigned to defile me in my dream, die, in the name of Jesus.
89. Every pharaoh of defilement, let me go, in the name of Jesus.
90. Every defilement, break, in the name of Jesus.
91. Ancestral contamination, defiling my destiny, be wiped off by the power in the blood of Jesus.
92. Every serpent and scorpion of defilement, that has entered into my dwelling place, die, in the name of Jesus.
93. Ladders of defilement, roast, in the name of Jesus.
94. Every defilement I've suffered as a baby, Holy Ghost fire, wipe it away, in the name of Jesus.
95. Every defilement I've suffered in the womb, Holy Ghost fire, wipe it away, in the name of Jesus.
96. Every defilement I've suffered in the dream, Holy Ghost fire, wipe it away, in the name of Jesus.

97. Every decision of darkness against my destiny, dry up by fire, in Jesus' name.
98. All the dark spirits on assignments against me, receive the blow of death, in the name of Jesus.
99. Father, by fire, transform my life, in the name of Jesus.
100. Holy Ghost fire, begin to arrest murmuring spirits in every department of my life, in the name of Jesus.
101. Holy Ghost fire, occupy every space vacated by evil arrows in me, in the name of Jesus.
102. Holy Ghost fire, revive my spiritual life, in Jesus' name
103. O Lord, let all quenchers of the fire of God in my life, be quenched by the fire of the Holy Ghost, in the name of Jesus
104. O Lord, let the fire of the Holy Ghost clear away every dirt from my spirit, in the name of Jesus
105. Holy Ghost fire, destroy every satanic garment made for my life, in the name of Jesus.

SECTION 2 DAY 6 (18-08-2015)

Confession Acts 2:17 And it shall come to pass in the last days, saith God, I will pour out of my Spirit upon all flesh: and your sons and your daughters shall prophesy, and your young men shall see visions, and your old men shall dream dreams:

Reading through the Bible in 70 Days (Day 16 - Judges 6:21 - 21:17)
Devotional Songs (Pages 11-14)
Praise Worship
Prayer of Praise and Thanksgiving (Pages 15 & 16)

106. Holy Ghost fire, boil spiritual contamination out of my blood, in Jesus' name.
107. Father, by fire by force, let me not surrender to the enemy, in Jesus' name.

108. Holy Ghost, arise and let me be the echo of Your Spirit, in the name of Jesus.
109. Holy Ghost, arise, let me be the trumpet of Your power, in the name of Jesus.
110. O God, arise in my spiritual life and let my enemies scatter, in Jesus' name.
111. O God, let my life be strengthened inside of me by fire by force, in the name of Jesus.
112. Father, renew my life in You, so that I will rejoice in You everyday of my life, in the name of Jesus.
113. By the fire of the Holy Ghost, I give an ejection order unto every evil stranger in my life, in the name of Jesus.
114. I unwind myself, from every evil that has settled around me, in Jesus' name.
115. Every yoke of unfriendly friend, break, in the name of Jesus.
116. I register my name, for visitation by angels of favour, in the name of Jesus.
117. I register the names of my enemies, for visitation by the angels of judgement, in the name of Jesus.
118. By fire, by force, let every infirmity fall away from my body, in Jesus' name.
119. O Lord, rebuild Your altar afresh in my life, in the name of Jesus.
120. O Lord, anoint my destiny afresh, in the name of Jesus.
121. Every power, attempting to build walls against my destiny, fall down and die, in the name of Jesus.
122. My soul, hear the word of the Lord, refuse to dwell in the hands of the tradition of my father's house, in the name of Jesus.
123. O God, arise extract me from covenants from the shrines of my forefathers, in the name of Jesus.
124. Holy Ghost fire, circulate all over my body, in the name of Jesus.
125. Holy Ghost, occupy every area vacated by spirit of uncertainty in my mind, in the name of Jesus.
126. I receive, the comforting anointing and power of the Holy Ghost, in the name of Jesus

MFM 2015 SEVENTY DAYS PRAYER & FASTING

SECTION 2 DAY 7 (19-08-2015)

Confession: Acts 2:17 And it shall come to pass in the last days, saith God, I will pour out of my Spirit upon all flesh: and your sons and your daughters shall prophesy, and your young men shall see visions, and your old men shall dream dreams:

Reading through the Bible in 70 Days (Day 17 - Jud 21:18-21:25; Ruth 1:1 - 4:22; 1Sam 1:1 - 15:4)

Devotional Songs (Pages 11-14)

Praise Worship

Prayer of Praise and Thanksgiving (Pages 15 & 16)

127. I receive, the unsearchable wisdom in the Holy Ghost, in the name of Jesus.
128. Holy Ghost fire, purge my life completely, in the name of Jesus.
129. Holy Ghost fire, fall upon my eyes and burn to ashes every evil force and all satanic power controlling my eyes, in Jesus' name.
130. Holy Ghost fire, destroy every satanic garment in my life, in Jesus' name.
131. Holy Ghost, grant me a glimpse of Your glory now, in Jesus' name.
132. Holy Ghost, quicken me, in the name of Jesus.
133. Holy Ghost, breathe on me now, in the name of Jesus.
134. Every thing that I've suffered in ignorance, fire of God, wipe it away, in the name of Jesus.
135. O Lord, let every old order that has taken advantage of me be wiped off, in the name of Jesus.
136. My Father, my Father, my Father, draw me out of the libation of my family line, in the name of Jesus.
137. Father, take my destiny away from the hands of evil men, in Jesus' name.
138. Every tree of manipulation, assigned against me shall not speak against me, in the name of Jesus.

139. By fire, by force, I call forth my life and my labour from the hands of the oppressors, in the name of Jesus.
140. When I prophesy unto the heavens, the heavens shall answer me, in the name of Jesus.
141. My priesthood, shall be binding in heaven and on earth, in the name of Jesus.
142. Holy Ghost fire, ordain me to reverse evil decrees, in the name of Jesus.
143. Any power, attempting to steal from my life, shall not go away unchecked, in the name of Jesus.
144. Every power that weakens my anointing, die, in the name of Jesus.
145. O God, arise by the thunder of Your power, and let every sorcery consultation against me be frustrated, in the name of Jesus.
146. I nullify, every legal document of the enemy assigned against me, in the name of Jesus.
147. I revoke, satanic certificate of occupancy of anything that belongs to me, in the name of Jesus.

SECTION 2 DAY 8 (20-08-2015)

Confession: Acts 2:17 And it shall come to pass in the last days, saith God, I will pour out of my Spirit upon all flesh: and your sons and your daughters shall prophesy, and your young men shall see visions, and your old men shall dream dreams:

Reading through the Bible in 70 Days (Day 18 - 1 Samuel 15:5-30:31)
Devotional Songs (Pages 11-14)
Praise Worship
Prayer of Praise and Thanksgiving (Pages 15 & 16)

148. By the power of the Holy Spirit and by the blood of Jesus, I reverse any mandate given to any evil power to supervise my life, in the name of Jesus.

149. Every deposit from the sun assigned to trouble me, I rebuke you, in the name of Jesus.
150. O sun, lift away your warfare from me right now, in the name of Jesus.
151. By the power that established the heaven and the earth, I decree every wall in my life to fall down and die, in the name of Jesus.
152. You moon, hear the word of the Lord, shut up your light with nigh traders, do not cooperate with them, in the name of Jesus.
153. Every power harbouring enchantments against me, vomit them, in the name of Jesus.
154. O sun, moon and stars, vomit every enchantment against my life, in the name of Jesus.
155. Every power that has marred the heavenlies for my sake, fall down and die, in the name of Jesus.
156. Holy Ghost fire, melt every bad spiritual deposit in my life, in Jesus' name.
157. Holy Ghost fire, cleanse my root from spiritual filth, in the name of Jesus.
158. Holy Ghost fire, melt every spiritual poison in my body, in the name of Jesus.
159. Holy Ghost Fire, burn in every department of my body and destroy every satanic deposit, in the name of Jesus.
160. O God, arise, set my spirit on Fire of the Holy Ghost, in the name of Jesus.
161. I charge my body, soul and spirit with the Fire of the Holy Ghost, in the name of Jesus.
162. Holy Ghost fire, quench every arrow of prayerlessness fired at me by the enemies of my soul, in the name of Jesus.
163. Anointing of the Holy Ghost, fall upon me and break every negative yoke, in the name of Jesus.
164. Holy Ghost fire, do the work of purification in my life, in the name of Jesus.
165. O Lord, ignite me with Your Holy Ghost fire, in the name of Jesus.

166. Holy Ghost fire, incubate my life with your freshness and refreshing power, in the name of Jesus.
167. Every power hiding in demonic holes against me, the Lord smite you there, in the name of Jesus.
168. Let the stars arise and begin to fight for me, in the name of Jesus.

SECTION 2 DAY 9 (21-08-2015)

Confession: Acts 2:17 And it shall come to pass in the last days, saith God, I will pour out of my Spirit upon all flesh: and your sons and your daughters shall prophesy, and your young men shall see visions, and your old men shall dream dreams:

Reading through the Bible in 70 Days (Day 19 -1Samuel 31:1-31:13; 2 Samuel 1:1-17:5)

Devotional Songs (Pages 11-14)

Praise Worship

Prayer of Praise and Thanksgiving (Pages 15 & 16)

169. O Lord, let the hired astral world assigned against me, cancel its assignment, in the name of Jesus.
170. Every power, wounding my soul shall not escape, in the name of Jesus.
171. Every conspiracy of the sun, moon and stars against me, O God, arise and scatter it, in the name of Jesus.
172. Every manipulation of the enemy against me, I nullify you by the power in the blood of Jesus, in the name of Jesus.
173. O sun, arise and smite every enemy of my soul, in the name of Jesus.
174. Father, let the spirit of prophecy, fall upon me, in the name of Jesus.
175. Holy Ghost, fill me that I might bring forth healing power, in Jesus' name.
176. Holy Ghost fire, destroy every garment of reproach in my life, in Jesus' name.

177. Father, let the fire of the Holy Ghost enter into my blood stream and cleanse my system, in the name of Jesus.
178. Holy Ghost, seal all my pockets that have demonic holes, in Jesus' name.
179. Holy Ghost fire, begin to melt away every satanic deposit in my life, in the name of Jesus
180. Holy Ghost fire, destroy all satanic poisons in my body, in the name of Jesus
181. Holy Ghost fire, dry up all sicknesses in my body, in the name of Jesus.
182. Holy Ghost fire, immunize my blood against satanic poisoning, in the name of Jesus.
183. Holy Ghost fire, melt away every spiritual blindness in my life, in the name of Jesus.
184. Holy Ghost, pump favour into my life, in the name of Jesus
185. Every dry bone of my spiritual life, receive the fire of the God of Elijah, in the name of Jesus.
186. Father, let Your power and Your glory, energise my spirit man, in the name of Jesus.
187. Every plantation of darkness, blocking my spiritual pipe, Holy Ghost fire, flush it out, in the name of Jesus.
188. My Father, my Father, my Father, let me experience the bulldozing power of the God of Elijah, in the name of Jesus.
189. I receive fire power, to tread upon serpents and scorpions and upon every power of the enemy, in the name of Jesus.

SECTION 2 DAY 10 (22-08-2015)

Confession: Acts 2:17 And it shall come to pass in the last days, saith God, I will pour out of my Spirit upon all flesh: and your sons and your daughters shall prophesy, and your young men shall see visions, and your old men shall dream dreams:

MFM 2015 SEVENTY DAYS PRAYER & FASTING

Reading through the Bible in 70 Days (Day 20 - 2Samuel 17:6-24:25; 1 Kings 1:1-6:3)

Devotional Songs (Pages 11-14)

Praise Worship

Prayer of Praise and Thanksgiving (Pages 15 & 16)

190. I receive fire power, to pursue and possess, in the name of Jesus.
191. Holy Ghost fire, fill my body, soul and spirit with the power of the Holy Spirit, in the name of Jesus.
192. Fire, that will convert my life to that of an environmental transformer, fall upon me now, in the name of Jesus.
193. Fire, that will empower me to kill all my problems and my enemies, fall upon me now, in the name of Jesus.
194. Holy Ghost fire, eliminate the blockages which have been arresting my blessings, in the name of Jesus.
195. By the power of the Holy Ghost, by the fire of the Holy Ghost, I will experience marathon favour and breakthroughs, in the name of Jesus.
196. By the power of the Holy Ghost, by the fire of the Holy, the Lord will accelerate me to a new place, in the name of Jesus.
197. Holy Ghost fire, burn away every seed of affliction arising from my foundation, in the name of Jesus.
198. Every arrow of shame, fired at my destiny, I terminate you now, in the name of Jesus.
199. My life, generate positive impact and miracle-working power of God, in the name of Jesus.
200. By the fire of the Holy Ghost, the Lord shall waste my wasters and my wasted years shall be compensated, in the name of Jesus.
201. Every arrangement of darkness, to frustrate and to discourage me, I command them to burn to ashes, in the name of Jesus.

202. Power of God, fall upon me mightily in a way that will embarrass the enemy, in the name of Jesus.
203. Holy Ghost and fire, fill my body, soul and spirit, in the name of Jesus.
204. Father, let me experience a personal Pentecost, in the name of Jesus.
205. Father, let Your glory shine upon my life, in the name of Jesus.
206. Every arrow of the oppressor, assigned to torment me, I burn you to ashes, in the name of Jesus.
207. Father, announce my name for greatness, in the name of Jesus.
208. Father, announce my name for great breakthroughs, in the name of Jesus.
209. Father, any glory stolen from my life, let Your fire restore it, in Jesus' name.
210. Spirit of the living God, overshadow my life by Your fire and power, and put all my enemies to flight, in the name of Jesus.

SECTION CONFESSIONS

God has equipped me, and made me a danger and a terror to all my enemies, in the name of Jesus. The Lord is my light and my salvation, whom shall I fear? The Lord is the strength of my life; of whom shall I be afraid? When the wicked, even mine enemies and foes, come upon me to eat up my flesh, they stumble and fall, in the name of Jesus. I pursue my enemies, I overtake and destroy them, in Jesus' name. The Lord has lifted me up and I am seated with Him in heavenly places in Christ Jesus, far above principalities, powers and dominion, and the Lord has put all things under my feet, and I use my feet to bruise and destroy all my enemies even satan, in the name of Jesus. In Jesus' name, anywhere the soles of my feet shall tread upon, the Lord has given it unto me.

The word of God is the power of God, and the entrance of the word of God into my life, has brought the light of God into my life and darkness cannot comprehend it, in the name of Jesus. I send forth this light that is in me as a two-edged sword to destroy all the kingdoms of darkness, in the name of Jesus. The word of God is quick and powerful in my mouth. God has put the power of His word in my mouth, in the name of Jesus. I trust in the word of God, the word stands sure when I speak it, it will accomplish the purpose for which I have spoken it, in Jesus' name.

SECTION VIGIL
(To be done at night between the hours of 12 midnight and 2am)
HYMN FOR THE VIGIL (Page 14)

1. My Father, break the teeth of the ungodly, in Jesus' name.
2. O Lord, hear my voice whenever I call, in the name of Jesus.
3. O God, visit every power lying against me with destruction, in Jesus' name.
4. O Lord, let the dry wind from heaven blow down the pillars of their confident buildings, in the name of Jesus.
5. Hot coals of fire from heaven, blow down their houses, in Jesus' name.
6. O Lord, let the enemies of this country, become merely another story told, in the name of Jesus.
7. My Father, let my enemies fall, by their own counsel, in Jesus' name.
8. By the word of God, many sorrows shall be to the wicked, in Jesus' name.
9. O God, command judgement on all my oppressors, in Jesus' name.
10. O Lord, let judgment and shame pursue the stubborn pursuers of this country and sweep away their powers, in the name of Jesus.
11. O Lord, let all weapons of the enemies of this country, backfire seven-fold on them, in the name of Jesus.
12. You enemies of this country, hear the word of the Lord, you are setting a trap for yourself, in the name of Jesus.
13. Let the wickedness of the wicked come to an end, O Lord, in Jesus' name.
14. O Lord, let Your anger boil against the wicked every day, in Jesus' name.
15. Every trap, that repeats evil circles, catch your owner, in Jesus' name.
16. Snare, of right place at the wrong time, break by fire, in Jesus' name.

17. Snare, of being one day late, one naira short, break, in the name of Jesus.
18. Snare, of too little, too late, break, in the name of Jesus.
19. Prayers of Jabez, to provoke my enlargement, manifest in my life, in the name of Jesus.
20. Every evil contract, signed by my ancestors in the heavenlies, catch fire, in Jesus' name.
21. Every dog, collar assigned to lead me astray, break, in the name of Jesus.

MFM 2015 SEVENTY DAYS PRAYER & FASTING

SECTION 3 -
PERSONAL PROPHECIES TO MOVE YOU FORWARD

Personalize each prophecy by confessing each seven times

Scripture Reading: Isaiah 6

Confession: Micah 7:8: Rejoice not against me, O mine enemy: when I fall, I shall arise; when I sit in darkness, the Lord shall be a light unto me.

SECTION 3 DAY 1 (23-08-2015)

Reading through the Bible in 70 Days (Day 21 - 1 Kings 6:4-18:3)
Devotional Songs (Pages 11-14)
Praise Worship
Prayer of Praise and Thanksgiving (Pages 14 & 15)

1. I shall not quench, the fire of the Holy Spirit, in the name of Jesus.
2. I am filled, with all the spiritual blessings in heavenly places, in Jesus' name.
3. I have, resurrection power within me, in the name of Jesus.
4. My words, are increasing in power and force, in the name of Jesus.
5. I possess, a merry heart that doeth good like medicine, in the name of Jesus.
6. God, has given me dominion, in the name of Jesus.
7. I shall cooperate with God, in the kind of life I should live, in the name of Jesus.
8. I am complete, in the Lord Jesus Christ, in the name of Jesus.
9. I speak and think, of whatever is of good report, in the name of Jesus.
10. My God, shall supply all my needs according to His riches in glory, in the name of Jesus.
11. I decree, divine acceleration and laughter into my life, in the name of Jesus.
12. Good news, bombard my life before the end of this year, in the name of Jesus.
13. Satanic serpents, dispatched against me, receive madness, in the name of Jesus.

MFM 2015 SEVENTY DAYS PRAYER & FASTING

14. Satanic serpents, dispatched against every member of my household, be paralyzed and roasted, in the name of Jesus.
15. All satanic parasites, assigned to my finances die, in the name of Jesus.
16. You the tongue, raining incantations on me dry up, in the name of Jesus.
17. Every hunter of my soul, shoot yourself, in the name of Jesus.
18. My heart, will not be a stony ground for the word of God, in the name of Jesus.
19. My heart, will not be a way side ground, in the name of Jesus.
20. My heart, will not be a ground of thorns, in the name of Jesus.
21. Mountains of confrontation, crumble, in the name of Jesus.

SECTION 3 DAY 2 (24-08-2015)

Confession: Micah 7:8: Rejoice not against me, O mine enemy: when I fall, I shall arise; when I sit in darkness, the Lord shall be a light unto me.

Reading through the Bible in 70 Days (Day 22 -1Kings 18:4-22:53; 2 Kings 1:1-9:33)

Devotional Songs (Pages 11-14)

Praise Worship

Prayer of Praise and Thanksgiving (Pages 15 & 16)

22. The Lord is my helper, I will not be afraid of what man can do to me.
23. The name of the Lord is a strong tower, I run into it and I am safe, in the name of Jesus.
24. I will not speak what comes to my mind, but will speak what is in God's mind, in the name of Jesus.
25. My faith, comes by hearing, as I listen to the word of God, in the name of Jesus.
26. The hand of the Lord is upon me; as I prophecy, great things happen, in the name of Jesus.

27. Though my outward man may be decaying, my inward man is renewed day by day, in the name of Jesus.
28. My youth, is renewed like the eagle. My eyes are not growing dim nor is my strength diminished, in the name of Jesus.
29. I hear, the sound of an abundance of the rain of blessing coming my way, in the name of Jesus.
30. I am a king, I reign in life through Jesus Christ.
31. My mockery, be converted to promotion, in the name of Jesus.
32. My mockery, be converted to success, in the name of Jesus.
33. You the sharp teeth and pit of the enemy, turn against the enemy, in the name of Jesus.
34. Those who do not know me will fight for my cause, in the name of Jesus.
35. You the handwriting of the enemy, turn against the enemy, in Jesus' name.
36. Every evil king, installed against me, be paralyzed, in the name of Jesus.
37. All strongholds of debt, be dashed to pieces, in the name of Jesus.
38. All strongholds of oppression, be dashed to pieces, in the name of Jesus.
39. All strongholds of infirmity, be dashed to pieces, in the name of Jesus.
40. All strongholds of curses and covenants, be dashed to pieces, in Jesus' name.
41. All strongholds of unprofitable efforts, be dashed to pieces, in Jesus' name.
42. Evil clouds over my head, blow away, in the name of Jesus.

SECTION 3 DAY 3 (25-08-2015)

Confession: Micah 7:8: Rejoice not against me, O mine enemy: when I fall, I shall arise; when I sit in darkness, the Lord shall be a light unto me.
Reading through the Bible in 70 Days (Day 23 - 2Kings 9:34-25:11)
Devotional Songs (Pages 11-14)
Praise Worship

MFM 2015 SEVENTY DAYS PRAYER & FASTING

Prayer of Praise and Thanksgiving (Pages 15 & 16)

43. I live by faith and not by sight, in the name of Jesus.
44. I tread, upon all serpents and scorpions, they cannot harm me, in Jesus' name.
45. I am divinely insured, no weapon fashioned against me shall prosper, in the name of Jesus.
46. I am blessed, with all spiritual blessings in the heavenlies, in the name of Jesus.
47. I make Jesus the great physician, my doctor, in the name of Jesus.
48. I forbid satan, to put any disease in my body, in the name of Jesus.
49. The joy of the Lord, is my strength, in the name of Jesus.
50. God's word, is life and health unto all my flesh, in the name of Jesus.
51. Every part of my body, functions perfectly, in the name of Jesus.
52. I use the power of God, to meet any need, in the name of Jesus.
53. Ancient gates, blocking my inheritance, catch fire, in the name of Jesus.
54. Any curse, affecting my brain, break by the power in the blood of Jesus.
55. Fire of affliction, die and rise no more, in the name of Jesus.
56. I sack every satanic checkpoint mounted against my success, in Jesus' name.
57. Deliverance, take place in my dream, in the name of Jesus.
58. Habitation of evil planners, turn upside down, in the name of Jesus.
59. All caged glories, be released, in the name of Jesus.
60. All spirit lions, delegated against me, be paralyzed, in the name of Jesus.
61. All spirit serpents, delegated against me, be paralyzed, in the name of Jesus.
62. All spirit scorpions, delegated against me, be paralyzed, in the name of Jesus.
63. All spirit dragons, delegated against me, be paralyzed, in the name of Jesus.

SECTION 3 DAY 4 (26-08-2015)

Confession: Micah 7:8: Rejoice not against me, O mine enemy: when I fall, I shall arise; when I sit in darkness, the Lord shall be a light unto me.

Reading through the Bible in 70 Days (Day 24 - 2Kings 25:12-25:30; 1 Chronicles 1:1-11:4)

Devotional Songs (Pages 11-14)

Praise Worship

Prayer of Praise and Thanksgiving (Pages 15 & 16)

64. I will not lack any good thing, in the name of Jesus.
65. I am blessed, so that I can be a blessing to others, in the name of Jesus.
66. I refuse to be poor, Christ has redeemed me from the curse of poverty, in the name of Jesus.
67. Poverty and lack, are underneath my feet, in the name of Jesus.
68. I am the head and not the tail, in the name of Jesus.
69. Wealth and riches, are in my house, in the name of Jesus
70. My faith, can come under tests, but I will pass the tests, in the name of Jesus.
71. I will not become bitter towards anyone, I will pray for those who slander me, in the name of Jesus.
72. I am an overcomer, because I live by faith and not by sight, in Jesus' name.
73. God, has not given me the spirit of fear, but of power, love and a sound mind, in the name of Jesus.
74. All enemies like the sun, be dismantled unto desolation, in the name of Jesus.
75. All enemies like the moon, be dismantled unto desolation, in Jesus' name.
76. I will rise, above the unbelievers around me, in the name of Jesus.
77. I bury my failures today, in the name of Jesus.
78. I disarm, every satanic king and his authority, in the name of Jesus.
79. My foundation, be strengthened to carry divine prosperity, in Jesus' name.

MFM 2015 SEVENTY DAYS PRAYER & FASTING

80. Riches of the ungodly, be transferred to me, in the name of Jesus.
81. Thunder from the Lord, destroy every evil altar constructed against my finances, in the name of Jesus.
82. Every chain of satanic delay, on my prosperity be shattered, in Jesus' name.
83. All my paralyzed potentials, receive the resurrection power of the Lord Jesus Christ, in the name of Jesus.
84. All my buried virtues, receive the resurrection power of the Lord Jesus Christ, in the name of Jesus.

SECTION 3 DAY 5 (27-08-2015)

Confession: Micah 7:8: Rejoice not against me, O mine enemy: when I fall, I shall arise; when I sit in darkness, the Lord shall be a light unto me.

Reading through the Bible in 70 Days (Day 25 -   1 Chronicles 11:5-27:12)

Devotional Songs (Pages 11-14)

Praise Worship

Prayer of Praise and Thanksgiving (Pages 15 & 16)

85. I have mountain-moving faith, I speak to mountains and they obey me, in the name of Jesus.
86. I do not fear the future, because I trust in God, in the name of Jesus.
87. I am, the property of the Lord Jesus Christ, in the name of Jesus.
88. I dwell, in the secret place of the Most High, in the name of Jesus.
89. The power of God, is in me; no foe can withstand me, in the name of Jesus.
90. The angels of the Lord, encamp around me and deliver me from every evil work, in the name of Jesus.
91. I am redeemed, from the curse of sickness and I refuse to accept its symptoms, in the name of Jesus.

92. No evil shall befall me, neither shall any plague or calamity come near my dwelling, in the name of Jesus.
93. The word of God, is medication and life to my flesh, in the name of Jesus.
94. I put on, the whole armour of God, and the shield of faith protects me from the fiery darts of the wicked, in the name of Jesus.
95. All my dead talents, receive the resurrection power of the Lord Jesus Christ, in the name of Jesus.
96. All my slow progress, receive the resurrection power of the Lord Jesus Christ, in the name of Jesus.
97. All my battered emotions, receive the resurrection power of the Lord Jesus Christ, in the name of Jesus.
98. All my amputated blessings, receive the resurrection power of the Lord Jesus Christ, in the name of Jesus.
99. I reject fainting spirit, in the name of Jesus.
100. Any demon, living inside members of my household depart now, in the name of Jesus.
101. Every untamed enemy of my prosperity, be tamed by the Holy Ghost, in the name of Jesus.
102. Blood of Jesus, rub off evil creams and ointments put upon my body, in the name of Jesus.
103. You my helpers, appear, my hindrance, disappear, in the name of Jesus.
104. The riches of the gentiles, come to me, in the name of Jesus.
105. Divine magnets of prosperity, be planted in my hands, in the name of Jesus.

SECTION 3 DAY 6 (28-08-2015)

Confession: Micah 7:8: Rejoice not against me, O mine enemy: when I fall, I shall arise; when I sit in darkness, the Lord shall be a light unto me.

MFM 2015 SEVENTY DAYS PRAYER & FASTING

Reading through the Bible in 70 Days (Day 26 - 1Chronicles 27:13- 29:30; 2 Chronicles 1:1- 18:23)

Devotional Songs (Pages 11-14)

Praise Worship

Prayer of Praise and Thanksgiving (Pages 15 & 16)

106. God keeps all my bones, and not one of them is broken, in the name of Jesus.
107. God redeems my soul, from the power of the grave, in the name of Jesus.
108. I have life and is my pathway, there is no death, in the name of Jesus.
109. I am released from the bondage of the fear of death. in the name of Jesus.
110. I cast my cares, upon the Lord because He cares for me, in the name of Jesus.
111. I have the glorious divine inheritance, working inside me, in Jesus' name.
112. I reject, every tradition that does not conform to the word of God, in the name of Jesus.
113. I shall not utter words, that would disrespect God's authority, in Jesus' name.
114. I shall breakthrough and not breakdown, in the name of Jesus.
115. The world, shall read of my rising and not of my falling, in the name of Jesus.
116. Divine magnet of prosperity, be planted in my house, in the name of Jesus.
117. O Lord, let there be a reverse transfer, of my satanically transferred wealth, in the name of Jesus.
118. Thunder and lightning of God, scatter witchcraft gathering, in Jesus' name.
119. No power, shall hurry me out of the earth before my time, in Jesus' name.
120. My years, shall not be wasted, in the name of Jesus.
121. My pocket, will not leak, in the name of Jesus.
122. Holy Ghost arise, wipe away my tears, in the name of Jesus.
123. Every arrow of darkness, against fired at my testimonies this year, go back to your senders, in the name of Jesus.
124. Every trap, set for my destiny, catch your owner, in the name of Jesus.

125. I cancel, the voice of weeping, I loose the voice of singing, in Jesus' name..
126. O God, arise and trouble my trouble, in the name of Jesus.

SECTION 3 DAY 7 (29-08-2015)

Confession: Micah 7:8: Rejoice not against me, O mine enemy: when I fall, I shall arise; when I sit in darkness, the Lord shall be a light unto me.

Reading through the Bible in 70 Days (Day 27 - 2 Chronicles 18:24 - 36:16)

Devotional Songs (Pages 11-14)

Praise Worship

Prayer of Praise and Thanksgiving (Pages 15 & 16)

127. I shall not roam aimlessly, in the market square of life, in the name of Jesus.
128. I will not drink, the water of affliction, in the name of Jesus.
129. My David, arise and kill your Goliath, in the name of Jesus.
130. I make God's word my word, in the name of Jesus.
131. I will walk, in love and by faith in God's word, in the name of Jesus.
132. All things are possible with God, and I choose to believe in Him, in the name of Jesus.
133. I release Christ in me, the hope of my glory, in the name of Jesus.
134. I have the keys, of the kingdom of God; whatever I bind is bound in heaven, whatever I loose is loosed in heaven, in the name of Jesus.
135. My success, is not dependent on luck or chance; it has to do with Jesus, in the name of Jesus.
136. I shall not die, but live to declare the glory of God, in the name of Jesus.
137. Expectations of my enemies, perish by fire, in the name of Jesus.
138. Every expectation of the wicked, concerning my destiny, die, in Jesus' name.
139. My Father, baptize me with uncommon mercy, in the name of Jesus.

140. Any plan of the enemy, to turn my light to darkness, scatter, in Jesus' name.
141. The finger that disgraced Pharaoh, disgrace my enemies, in Jesus' name.
142. Finger of God, arm of God, arise re-write my family history, in Jesus' name.
143. Every end of the year activity, of the enemy, receive confusion, in the name of Jesus.
144. Where is the Lord God of Elijah, take me from mockery to honor, in the name of Jesus.
145. I take back, all the breakthrough keys the enemy has stolen from me, in the name of Jesus.
146. I break down, the stronghold of witchcraft in my family, in the name of Jesus.
147. Secrets of strange children, in my family, be revealed, in the name of Jesus.

SECTION 3 DAY 8 (30-08-2015)

Confession: Micah 7:8: Rejoice not against me, O mine enemy: when I fall, I shall arise; when I sit in darkness, the Lord shall be a light unto me.

Reading through the Bible in 70 Days (Day 28 - 2Chronicles 36:17- 36:23; Ezra 1:1 - 10:44; Nehemiah 1:1 - 7:33)

Devotional Songs (Pages 11-14)

Praise Worship

Prayer of Praise and Thanksgiving (Pages 15 & 16)

148. I am fulfilling, God's plan for my life, in the name of Jesus
149. I bind, every desert spirit, in the name of Jesus.
150. I cancel, every bewitchment fashioned against my destiny, in Jesus' name.
151. O Lord, let Your fire destroy every satanic weapon fashioned against my destiny, in the name of Jesus.
152. Lord, expose all satanic schemes devised against my destiny, in Jesus' name.
153. I reclaim, all the grounds I have lost to the enemy, in the name of Jesus.

154. I paralyse, every satanic ammunition, in the name of Jesus.
155. I paralyse, every unrepentant opposition, in the name of Jesus.
156. I refuse to cooperate, with the enemy of my progress, in the name of Jesus.
157. I paralyze, all satanic strugglers, in the name of Jesus.
158. Every distance, stolen from my life by the enemy, I repossess you, in the name of Jesus.
159. Power of delayed blessings, die, in the name of Jesus.
160. All graves dug for me, swallow your diggers, in the name of Jesus.
161. Holy Ghost, explode in my life by signs and wonders, in the name of Jesus.
162. Evil hands, pointed at me, dry up, in the name of Jesus.
163. By the power, that divided the Red Sea, let my problems die, in Jesus' name.
164. Every evil river, in my place of birth, release my virtues, in the name of Jesus.
165. O Lord, find the dragon in my life and kill it, in the name of Jesus.
166. I smash serpentine heads, reared against me into pieces, in Jesus' name.
167. I break, every evil hold on my breakthroughs, in the name of Jesus.
168. I paralyse, every anti-breakthrough strategy, in the name of Jesus.

SECTION 3 DAY 9 (31-08-2015)

Confession: Micah 7:8: Rejoice not against me, O mine enemy: when I fall, I shall arise; when I sit in darkness, the Lord shall be a light unto me.

Reading through the Bible in 70 Days (Day 29 - Neh 7:34 - 13:31; Esther 1:1 - 10:3; Job 1:1 - 2:6)

Devotional Songs (Pages 11-14)

Praise Worship

Prayer of Praise and Thanksgiving (Pages 15 & 16)

169. I scatter, all forces encamping against me, in the name of Jesus.

170. I paralyse, every instrument of oppression fashioned against me, in the name of Jesus.
171. Spirit of pains and sorrows, be bound, in the name of Jesus.
172. Evil spies, searching for my secrets, be paralyzed, in the name of Jesus.
173. Every unprofitable alliance against me, scatter, in the name of Jesus.
174. I arrest, every problem in my life from the root, in the name of Jesus.
175. O God, arise and give me a turnaround breakthrough, in the name of Jesus.
176. Every curse, working against my destiny, break, in the name of Jesus.
177. In my finances, O Lord, give me the divine ability to overtake those who have gone ahead, in the name of Jesus.
178. O Lord, lead me to those who will bless me, in the name of Jesus.
179. My Father, lead me away from those assigned to demote me, in Jesus' name.
180. My Father, lead me away from unfriendly friends and friendly demoters, in the name of Jesus.
181. O Lord, let my breakthrough frustrate the plans of the enemy, in the name of Jesus.
182. Evil effect of cursed-house and land, upon my property, break by fire, in the name of Jesus.
183. Every cycle, of financial turbulence, break by the power in the blood of Jesus.
184. Woe, unto every vessel of poverty pursuing me, in the name of Jesus.
185. I smash, the poverty serpents on the wall of fire, in the name of Jesus.
186. I set, every garment of poverty on fire, in the name of Jesus.
187. Every identification mark of poverty, upon my life, be rubbed off by the blood of Jesus, in the name of Jesus.
188. Every identification mark of witchcraft, upon my life, be rubbed off by the blood of Jesus, in the name of Jesus.
189. I withdraw my wealth, from the hand of the bondwoman and her children, in the name of Jesus.

SECTION 3 DAY 10 (01-09-2015)

Confession: Micah 7:8: Rejoice not against me, O mine enemy: when I fall, I shall arise; when I sit in darkness, the Lord shall be a light unto me.

Reading through the Bible in 70 Days (Day 30 - Job 2:7 - 20:15)

Devotional Songs (Pages 11-14)

Praise Worship

Prayer of Praise and Thanksgiving (Pages 15 & 16)

190. My Father, embarrass me with abundance, in the name of Jesus.
191. I receive, the anointing to disgrace satanic arrows of poverty, in Jesus' name.
192. I cut off, every supply of food to my problems, in the name of Jesus.
193. Lord, release me from known and unknown financial curses, in Jesus' name.
194. I rebuke, every power working against the soundness of my finances, in the name of Jesus.
195. I seal the rebuke, with the blood of Jesus.
196. I break, every evil padlock put upon my finances, in the name of Jesus.
197. Blood of Jesus, flush out and scatter witchcraft meetings summoned against my wealth, in the name of Jesus.
198. Every satanic resistance, to my breakthroughs, crumble, in Jesus' name.
199. By the power in the blood of Jesus, I will become all that God created me to be, in the name of Jesus.
200. Every good area in my life, that the enemies has denied expression, receive resurrection, in the name of Jesus.
201. I receive, the resurrection power of the Lord Jesus Christ for my wealth to manifest, in the name of Jesus.
202. Every roar of satanic lions against my life, be silenced by fire, in Jesus' name.
203. Activities of vagabond evil broadcasters, be terminated by fire, in the name of Jesus.

204. Every satanic pregnancy, against my life, be aborted by fire, in Jesus' name.
205. Every power, hunting for my secrets, be deaf and blind, in the name of Jesus.
206. I paralyse, every power of bewitchment fashioned against me, in the name of Jesus.
207. Every spirit of pocket with holes, be disgraced out of my life, in Jesus' name.
208. All evil rivers, flowing down to me, from my father and mother, dry up, in the name of Jesus.
209. I quench, the power of star paralyzers, in the name of Jesus.
210. Every power, swallowing the results of my prayers, fall down and die, in the name of Jesus.

SECTION CONFESSIONS

Who is like unto Him, our God, who dwells on high, far above all powers and dominions. He raiseth up the poor out of the dust, and lifteth the needy out of the dunghill; that He might set him with princes. Even so shall the Lord deal with me, in the name of Jesus. The Bible says, that whatsoever I desire when I pray, I should believe and receive, in the name of Jesus. Therefore, I pray now that, in Jesus' name, I am set free from every captivity or attack of negative speech from my mouth or thoughts and from my heart, against myself. I tear down, in faith, every spiritual wall of partition, between me and my divinely appointed helpers and benefactors, in the name of Jesus.

In the name of Jesus Christ, the mighty hand of God is upon my life, upholding and protecting me from all who rise up against me, in the name of Jesus. Jesus Christ has made His grace available to me. I ask for the grace and I receive it by faith, in the name of Jesus. I can do and possess all things, through Christ who strengthens me. And my God shall supply all my needs, according to His riches in glory by Christ Jesus. My heart, is from now comforted, for the God of suddenly, provision and grace is still on the throne, in the name of Jesus.

SECTION VIGIL
(To be done at night between the hours of 12 midnight and 2am)
HYMN FOR THE VIGIL (Page 14)

1. Though, war should rise against me, in this will I be confident, in Jesus' name.
2. And now, shall my head be lifted up above my enemies round about me, in the name of Jesus.
3. O Lord, deliver me not over unto the will of mine enemies, in Jesus' name.
4. Divine raging storms, locate any coven assigned to bury the destiny of this country, in the name of Jesus.
5. O God, release Your wrath upon every power of witchcraft troubling my destiny, in the name of Jesus.
6. O God, arise and root them out of their land in Your anger, in Jesus' name.
7. O God, arise, cast Your fury upon agents of affliction troubling my star, in Jesus' name.
8. O Lord, let the way of the oppressor be dark and slippery and let the angel of the Lord persecute them, in the name of Jesus.
9. O Lord, let destruction, come upon my enemies unawares and the net that they have hidden catch them, in Jesus' name.
10. O Lord, let the enemy, fall into the destruction he has created, in Jesus' name.
11. O Lord, let not them, that are my enemies wrongfully rejoice over me, in the name of Jesus.
12. Father, let my enemies be ashamed, and brought to confusion, together with those who rejoice at my hurt, in the name of Jesus.
13. O Lord, let my enemies be clothed with shame, in the name of Jesus.
14. Stir up Thineself, O Lord, and fight for me, in Jesus' name.
15. Every evil altar, erected for our country, be disgraced, in Jesus' name.
16. O Lord, let the thunder of God, smite every evil priest working against our country at the evil altar and burn them to ashes, in the name of Jesus.

17. Every ancestral secret, retarding my progress, be revealed, in Jesus' name.
18. Evil secret activities, currently affecting my life, be exposed and disgraced, in the name of Jesus.
19. Every secret, I need to know to excel spiritually and financially, be revealed, in the name of Jesus.
20. Every secret, hidden in the marine kingdom, affecting my elevation, be exposed and disgraced, in the name of Jesus.
21. Every secret, hidden in the satanic archive, crippling my elevation, be exposed and disgraced, in the name of Jesus.

MFM 2015 SEVENTY DAYS PRAYER & FASTING

SECTION 4 -
DELIVERANCE OF THE HEAD, HAND AND FEET

Scripture Reading: Genesis 49

Confessions: Psalms 92:10 But my horn shalt thou exalt like the horn of an unicorn: I shall be anointed with fresh oil.

Luke 10:19 Behold, I give unto you power to tread on serpents and scorpions, and over all the power of the enemy: and nothing shall by any means hurt you.

Psalms 144:1 Blessed be the Lord my strength, which teacheth my hands to war, and my fingers to fight:

SECTION 4 DAY 1 (02-09-2015)

Reading through the Bible in 70 Days (Day 31 - Job 20:16 - 37:16)
Devotional Songs (Pages 11-14)
Praise Worship
Prayer of Praise and Thanksgiving (Pages 15 & 16)

1. Evil hands, anointed to waste my head, wither, in the name of Jesus.
2. Every arrow of untimely death, fired into my brain, backfire, in Jesus' name.
3. My head, my head, my head, hear the word of the Lord, arise and shine, in the name of Jesus.
4. Any dark invisible cover, on my head, catch fire, in the name of Jesus.
5. Every curse, operating against my head, die by the power in the blood of Jesus, in Jesus' name.
6. Every manipulation of my glory, through my hair, scatter now, in Jesus' name.
7. Every hand of the strongman, upon my head, dry up, in the name of Jesus.
8. Every power of death, assigned against my head, die, in the name of Jesus.
9. Chains upon my head, break, in the name of Jesus.
10. Holy Ghost fire arise, kill every satanic deposit in my head, in Jesus' name.

11. My head, receive deliverance by fire, in the name of Jesus.
12. Every power, summoning my head from the gate of the grave, die, in the name of Jesus.
13. Thou power of God, arise, attack all covens assigned against my head, in the name of Jesus.
14. Every ordinance, invoked by the power of darkness into the heavens against my head, I wipe you off, in the name of Jesus.
15. Rain of wisdom, knowledge and favour, fall upon my head, in Jesus' name.
16. Voices of strangers, casting spells against my head, die, in the name of Jesus.
17. Blood of Jesus, water of life, fire of God, wash my head, in the name of Jesus.
18. I shake off, bullets of darkness from my head, in the name of Jesus.
19. Every power, using my hair against me, die, in the name of Jesus.
20. Invisible loads of darkness, upon my head, catch fire, in the name of Jesus.
21. My head, my head, receive the touch of the resurrection power of the Lord Jesus Christ, in the name of Jesus.

SECTION 4 DAY 2 (03-09-2015)

Confessions: Psalms 92:10 But my horn shalt thou exalt like the horn of an unicorn: I shall be anointed with fresh oil.
Luke 10:19 Behold, I give unto you power to tread on serpents and scorpions, and over all the power of the enemy: and nothing shall by any means hurt you.
Psalms 144:1 Blessed be the Lord my strength, which teacheth my hands to war, and my fingers to fight:
Reading through the Bible in 70 Days (Day 32-Job 37:17- 42:17; Psalms 1:1-22:25)
Devotional Songs (Pages 11-14)
Praise Worship

MFM 2015 SEVENTY DAYS PRAYER & FASTING

Prayer of Praise and Thanksgiving (Pages 15 & 16)

22. Every arrow, fired into my head, go back to the sender, in the name of Jesus.
23. I decree, that insanity is not my lot, so every arrow of insanity, go back to the sender, in the name of Jesus.
24. My head, be lifted up above my enemies around me, in the name of Jesus.
25. My head, be lifted up above all the unbelievers around me, in Jesus' name..
26. My head, hear the word of the Lord, arise, possess your possessions and posses your destiny, in the name of Jesus.
27. Every handwriting of darkness, working against my head, backfire, in the name of Jesus.
28. I plug my head, into the resurrection power of the Lord Jesus Christ, in the name of Jesus.
29. I plug my hands, into the resurrection power of the Lord Jesus Christ, in the name of Jesus.
30. I plug my feet, into the resurrection power of the Lord Jesus Christ, in the name of Jesus.
31. I plug my head, into the socket of divine favour, in the name of Jesus.
32. I plug my hands, into the socket of divine favour, in the name of Jesus.
33. I plug my feet, into the socket of divine favour, in the name of Jesus.
34. Every curse, assigned against my head, disappear, in the name of Jesus.
35. Every evil cap, of my parents, will not fit my head, in the name of Jesus.
36. My hands, receive the fire to prosper, in the name of Jesus.
37. My hands, reject every pollution, in the name of Jesus.
38. Every arrow fired to downgrade my hands, I send you back to the senders, in the name of Jesus.
39. Every authority of darkness, assigned to paralyse my hands, die, in the name of Jesus.

40. My hands, reject every arrow of weakness and every arrow of sadness, in the name of Jesus.
41. My hands, become the weapons of war, in the name of Jesus.
42. O God, arise and convert my hands to Your battle axe, in the name of Jesus.

SECTION 4 DAY 3 (04-09-2015)

Confessions: Psalms 92:10 But my horn shalt thou exalt like the horn of an unicorn: I shall be anointed with fresh oil.

Luke 10:19 Behold, I give unto you power to tread on serpents and scorpions, and over all the power of the enemy: and nothing shall by any means hurt you.

Psalms 144:1 Blessed be the Lord my strength, which teacheth my hands to war, and my fingers to fight:

Reading through the Bible in 70 Days (Day 33 - Psalms 22:26 - 50:5)

Devotional Songs (Pages 11-14)

Praise Worship

Prayer of Praise and Thanksgiving (Pages 15 & 16)

43. O God, arise and convert my hands to Your weapons of war, in Jesus' name.
44. Father, I decree that every good thing I lay my hands upon, shall prosper by the power in the blood of Jesus.
45. Every sluggishness upon my hands, be shaken off by the power in the blood of Jesus.
46. My legs, receive the power of dominion, in the name of Jesus.
47. My feet, take me to my place of breakthrough, by the power in the blood of Jesus.
48. My feet, take me to my place of divine assignment, by the power in the blood of Jesus.

49. Every arrow of bad luck, fired at my feet, go back to your senders, in the name of Jesus.
50. Everywhere, the soles of my feet shall tread, heaven will take dominion, in the name of Jesus.
51. Wherever I walk in, darkness shall walk out, by the power in the blood of Jesus.
52. I receive the power, to disgrace every leg pollution, in the name of Jesus.
53. Father, anoint my feet for uncommon speed, in the name of Jesus.
54. Father, anoint my feet for uncommon success, in the name of Jesus.
55. By the spirit of the prophet, I move forward by fire, in the name of Jesus.
56. By the spirit of the prophet, I take dominion over every wickedness, in the name of Jesus.
57. Holy Ghost, anoint my legs for uncommon success, in the name of Jesus.
58. Holy Ghost, anoint my head, my hands, my legs, for uncommon testimonies, in the name of Jesus.
59. Father, I fire back, every arrow of sluggishness assigned to my feet, in the name of Jesus.
60. Anywhere I go, favour will be assigned to my feet, in the name of Jesus.
61. O Lord, let my feet be beautiful and bring glad tidings anywhere I go, in the name of Jesus.
62. Spirit of bad feet, backfire, in the name of Jesus.
63. Spirit of polluted feet, backfire, in the name of Jesus.

SECTION 4 DAY 4 (05-09-2015)

Confessions: Psalms 92:10 But my horn shalt thou exalt like the horn of an unicorn: I shall be anointed with fresh oil.

Luke 10:19 Behold, I give unto you power to tread on serpents and scorpions, and over all the power of the enemy: and nothing shall by any means hurt you.

MFM 2015 SEVENTY DAYS PRAYER & FASTING

Psalms 144:1 Blessed be the Lord my strength, which teacheth my hands to war, and my fingers to fight:

Reading through the Bible in 70 Days (Day 34 -   Psalms 50:6 - 78:4)

Devotional Songs (Pages 11-14)

Praise Worship

Prayer of Praise and Thanksgiving (Pages 15 & 16)

64. Every curse, issued against my legs, break, in the name of Jesus.
65. Every agenda of darkness, assigned to terrorise my legs, I fire it back, in the name of Jesus.
66. Holy Ghost, overshadow my head, in the name of Jesus.
67. Holy Ghost, overshadow my feet, in the name of Jesus.
68. Holy Ghost, overshadow my hands, in the name of Jesus.
69. Holy Ghost, overshadow every part of my body, in the name of Jesus.
70. Father, by the power that breaks yokes, let every yoke upon my head, be broken, in the name of Jesus.
71. Father, by the power that breaks yokes, let every yoke upon my hands, be broken, in the name of Jesus.
72. Father, by the power that breaks yokes, let every yoke upon my legs, be broken, in the name of Jesus.
73. Every handwriting of darkness, upon my head, I wipe you off by the power in the blood of Jesus.
74. Every handwriting of darkness, upon my hands, I wipe you off by the power in the blood of Jesus.
75. Every handwriting of darkness, upon my legs, I wipe you off by the power in the blood of Jesus.
76. Holy Ghost fire, pursue every danger out of my head, in the name of Jesus.
77. Holy Ghost fire, pursue every poison out of my head, in the name of Jesus.
78. Holy Ghost fire, pursue every poison out of my hands, in the name of Jesus.

79. Holy Ghost fire, pursue every poison out of my feet, in the name of Jesus.
80. I soak my head, I soak my hands, I soak my feet in the blood of Jesus.
81. Any problem, brought to my life through head attacks, die, in Jesus' name.
82. Powers of my father's house, release my head by fire, in the name of Jesus.
83. Serpents and scorpions, assigned against my head, die, in the name of Jesus.
84. I reject, the spirit of the tail and I claim the spirit of the head, in Jesus' name.

SECTION 4 DAY 5 (06-09-2015)

Confessions: Psalms 92:10 But my horn shalt thou exalt like the horn of an unicorn: I shall be anointed with fresh oil.

Luke 10:19 Behold, I give unto you power to tread on serpents and scorpions, and over all the power of the enemy: and nothing shall by any means hurt you.

Psalms 144:1 Blessed be the Lord my strength, which teacheth my hands to war, and my fingers to fight:

Reading through the Bible in 70 Days (Day 35 - Psalms 78:5 - 103:12)
Devotional Songs (Pages 11-14)
Praise Worship
Prayer of Praise and Thanksgiving (Pages 15 & 16)

85. I cancel, the power of all curses upon my head, in the name of Jesus.
86. Every witchcraft name, be dissolved from my fore-head and navel, in the name of Jesus.
87. Spiritual bat and spiritual lizard, that have been programmed into my head, receive the fire of God, in the name of Jesus.
88. My head, reject the covenant of failure, in the name of Jesus.
89. My head (lay your right hand on your forehead), from now on, life shall be easy for you. You shall be desired, appreciated and rewarded, in the name of Jesus.
90. None, shall pluck my stars out of my head, in the name of Jesus

91. I challenge, every marine hair on my head with the fire of God, and I command it to catch fire now, in the name of Jesus
92. My head, reject every manipulation and bewitchment of untimely death, in the name of Jesus.
93. Holy Ghost, crown my head and life with divine glory, in the name of Jesus.
94. O God, be my glory and the lifter up of my head, in Jesus' name.
95. And now, my head shall be lifted up above my enemies round about me, in the name of Jesus
96. I release my head, from every evil blood covenant, in the name of Jesus
97. Every power, that has formed any evil cloud over my head, scatter, in the name of Jesus.
98. Any evil umbrella, covering my head, scatter, in the name of Jesus.
99. Holy Ghost, hook my head unto my divine destiny, in the name of Jesus.
100. Fire of God, consume every strange satanic material in my head, in the name of Jesus.
101. O Lord, anoint my head with Your oil, bless my water and bread to eat of the fat of this land, in Jesus' name.
102. Every evil head, raised to suppress me, I pull you down by the power of the God of Elijah, in the name of Jesus.
103. Blood of Jesus, speak life into my head, my heart, my liver, my kidney, my bladder, my womb, etc, in the name of Jesus.
104. Any power, calling for my head before evil mirrors, die with the mirror, in the name of Jesus.
105. My glory, my head, arise and shine, in the name of Jesus.

SECTION 4 DAY 6 (07-09-2015)

Confessions: Psalms 92:10 But my horn shalt thou exalt like the horn of an unicorn: I shall be anointed with fresh oil.

MFM 2015 SEVENTY DAYS PRAYER & FASTING

Luke 10:19 Behold, I give unto you power to tread on serpents and scorpions, and over all the power of the enemy: and nothing shall by any means hurt you.
Psalms 144:1 Blessed be the Lord my strength, which teacheth my hands to war, and my fingers to fight:

Reading through the Bible in 70 Days (Day 36 -   Psalms 103:13 - 119:107)
Devotional Songs (Pages 11-14)
Praise Worship
Prayer of Praise and Thanksgiving (Pages 15 & 16)

106. Any power, calling my head for evil, scatter, in the name of Jesus
107. I fire back, every arrow of witchcraft in my head, in the name of Jesus.
108. Every evil hand, laid upon my head when I was a little child, die, in the name of Jesus.
109. My head, reject every bewitchment, in the name of Jesus.
110. Arrows of darkness, fired into my brain, die, in the name of Jesus.
111. Power of household wickedness, upon my brain, die, in the name of Jesus.
112. My head, reject every bewitchment, in the name of Jesus.
113. My brain, wake up by fire, in the name of Jesus.
114. Any power, calling my head for evil, scatter, in the name of Jesus.
115. I fire back, every arrow of witchcraft in my head, in the name of Jesus.
116. Holy Ghost fire, incubate my brain, in the name of Jesus.
117. Thou creative power of God, fall upon my brain now, in the name of Jesus.
118. Anything stolen from my brain, when I was a child, I repossess you now, in the name of Jesus
119. You grave, holding my head and its success captive, open up and vomit them to me by fire, in the name of Jesus.
120. You my dead and decayed head, resurrect and become perfectly healed and successful, in the name of Jesus.

121. You my head, that has been rendered useless, succeed by fire, in the name of Jesus.
122. You scorpions, assigned against my head, release me and die by fire, in the name of Jesus.
123. You evil arrows, fashioned against my head, I command you to go back to your senders, in the name of Jesus.
124. You spiritual worms, assigned to devour my head, come out and die, in the name of Jesus.
125. You spiritual devourers, assigned to devour my head and render it a living failure, come out and die, in the name of Jesus.
126. You evil objects, buried against the fruitfulness of my head, be up-rooted and scatter by fire, in the name of Jesus.

SECTION 4 DAY 7 (08-09-2015)

Confessions: Psalms 92:10 But my horn shalt thou exalt like the horn of an unicorn: I shall be anointed with fresh oil.

Luke 10:19 Behold, I give unto you power to tread on serpents and scorpions, and over all the power of the enemy: and nothing shall by any means hurt you.

Psalms 144:1 Blessed be the Lord my strength, which teacheth my hands to war, and my fingers to fight:

Reading through the Bible in 70 Days (Day 37 - Psalms 119:108-150:6; Proverbs 1:1-2:16)

Devotional Songs (Pages 11-14)

Praise Worship

Prayer of Praise and Thanksgiving (Pages 15 & 16)

127. You evil personalities, hiding in my head and causing it to fail, come out and die, in the name of Jesus.

128. You evil trenches, housing enemy ambush against my head, bury my enemies alive, in the name of Jesus.
129. Evil contractors, hired against my head, I terminate your contracts from source by fire, die, in the name of Jesus.
130. You spirit of hindrance, hindering my head from being crowned, release it and die, in the name of Jesus.
131. You spirit of hindrance, hindering my head from attaining fame and promotion, release it and die, in the name of Jesus.
132. You spirit of hindrance, preventing my head from acquiring her birthright, release it and die, in the name of Jesus.
133. Foreign witchcraft powers, co-operating with household witchcraft against my head, scatter and die, in the name of Jesus.
134. Household witchcraft, gathering against my head, scatter and die, in the name of Jesus.
135. Household witchcraft verdict, and conclusion against my head, be nullified by fire, in the name of Jesus.
136. Witchcraft covens, linked to the problems of my head, catch fire and scatter, in the name of Jesus.
137. You evil objects, being used to monitor my head for evil, be scattered and rendered invalid, in the name of Jesus.
138. You evil priests, ministering against my head from any evil altar, fall down and die, in the name of Jesus.
139. You evil altars, erected against the promotion and prominence of my head, be up-rooted and scatter, in the name of Jesus.
140. I pursue, I overtake and I recover by fire, whatever the enemy has stolen from my head, in the name of Jesus.
141. My head, defy any spiritual call to death or failure, in the name of Jesus.
142. My head, refuse to co-operate with my enemies against me, in the name of Jesus.

143. My head, always prevail and excel, in the name of Jesus.
144. You powers, manipulating my head, scatter and die by fire, in Jesus' name.
145. Every household witchcraft power, fall down and die, in the name of Jesus.
146. Every waster of my prosperity, become impotent, in the name of Jesus.
147. Every known and unknown aggressor, of my comfort, be paralyzed, in the name of Jesus.

SECTION 4 DAY 8 (09-09-2015)

Confessions: Psalms 92:10 But my horn shalt thou exalt like the horn of an unicorn: I shall be anointed with fresh oil:
Luke 10:19 Behold, I give unto you power to tread on serpents and scorpions, and over all the power of the enemy: and nothing shall by any means hurt you.
Psalms 144:1 Blessed be the Lord my strength, which teacheth my hands to war, and my fingers to fight:
Reading through the Bible in 70 Days (Day 38 - Proverbs 2:17-17:20)
Devotional Songs (Pages 11-14)
Praise Worship
Prayer of Praise and Thanksgiving (Pages 15 & 16)

148. Anything planted into my life, to disgrace me, come out with all your roots, in the name of Jesus.
149. I reject, demonic stagnation of my blessings, in the name of Jesus.
150. I reject, weak financial breakthroughs and claim big financial breakthroughs, in the name of Jesus.
151. Hidden and clever devourers, be bound, in the name of Jesus.
152. I release myself, from every evil family pattern of poverty, in Jesus' name.
153. I refuse, to allow my wealth to die on any evil altar, in the name of Jesus.
154. I reject, every prosperity paralysis, in the name of Jesus.

155. I possess, all my foreign benefits, in the name of Jesus.
156. I dash, every poverty dreams to the ground, in the name of Jesus.
157. My hands, have started to build and shall finish it, in the name of Jesus.
158. I refuse, to become the foot mat of amputators, in the name of Jesus.
159. God of providence, raise divine capital for me, in the name of Jesus.
160. I occupy, my rightful position, in the name of Jesus.
161. Every delayed and denied prosperity, manifest by fire, in Jesus' name.
162. Every bewitched account, receive deliverance, in the name of Jesus.
163. Every snail anointing, on my blessings, fall down and die, in Jesus' name.
164. Every power, broadcasting my goodness for evil, be silenced, in the name of Jesus.
165. I refuse, to lock the doors of blessings against myself, in Jesus' name.
166. I release myself, from every spirit of poverty, in the name of Jesus.
167. I curse, the spirit of poverty, in the name of Jesus.
168. I release myself, from every bondage of poverty, in the name of Jesus.

SECTION 4 DAY 9 (10-09-2015)

Confessions: Psalms 92:10 But my horn shalt thou exalt like the horn of an unicorn: I shall be anointed with fresh oil.

Luke 10:19 Behold, I give unto you power to tread on serpents and scorpions, and over all the power of the enemy: and nothing shall by any means hurt you.

Psalms 144:1 Blessed be the Lord my strength, which teacheth my hands to war, and my fingers to fight:

Reading through the Bible in 70 Days (Day 39 -Proverbs 17:21-31:31; Ecclesiastes 1:1-2:4)

Devotional Songs (Pages 11-14)

Praise Worship

MFM 2015 SEVENTY DAYS PRAYER & FASTING

Prayer of Praise and Thanksgiving (Pages 15 & 16)

169. I retrieve my purse, from the hand of Judas, in the name of Jesus.
170. I take over, the wealth of the sinner, in the name of Jesus.
171. I recover, the steering wheel of my wealth from the hands of evil drivers, in the name of Jesus.
172. Holy Ghost fire, revive my blessings, in the name of Jesus.
173. Holy Ghost fire, return my stolen blessings, in the name of Jesus.
174. O Lord, send out God's angels to bring me blessings, in the name of Jesus.
175. Whatever, needs changing in my life to bring the blessings, be changed now, in the name of Jesus.
176. Father, uncover to me, the key for prosperity, in the name of Jesus.
177. Every power, sitting on my wealth, fall down and die, in the name of Jesus.
178. Every power, of failure at the edge of success, die, in the name of Jesus.
179. Thou power of poor finishing, die, in the name of Jesus.
180. Heavenly fire, attack the power of poverty in my life, in the name of Jesus.
181. I overthrow, my strongman that troubled me this year, in Jesus' name.
182. Every habitation of wickedness, around me, be desolate, in Jesus' name.
183. Crystal ball and mirror of darkness, working against me, break, in the name of Jesus.
184. All round success, pursue and locate me, in the name of Jesus.
185. Father Lord, make my life a success story, in the name of Jesus.
186. Every satanic decree, against my life, die, in the name of Jesus.
187. I throw confusion, into the camp of my enemy, in the name of Jesus.
188. I get to my destiny, at the appointed time, in the name of Jesus.
189. I refuse to rotate, roam and circulate on the same spot, in Jesus' name.

MFM 2015 SEVENTY DAYS PRAYER & FASTING

SECTION 4 DAY 10 (11-09-2015)

Confessions: Psalms 92:10 But my horn shalt thou exalt like the horn of an unicorn: I shall be anointed with fresh oil.

Luke 10:19 Behold, I give unto you power to tread on serpents and scorpions, and over all the power of the enemy: and nothing shall by any means hurt you.

Psalms 144:1 Blessed be the Lord my strength, which teacheth my hands to war, and my fingers to fight:

Reading through the Bible in 70 Days (Day 40 - Ecclesiastes 2:5-12:14; Song of Solomon 1:1 - 8:14; Isaiah 1:1 - 6:12)

Devotional Songs (Pages 11-14)

Praise Worship

Prayer of Praise and Thanksgiving (Pages 15 & 16)

190. I withdraw my name, from the register of frustrations, in Jesus' name.
191. I prophesy to you my spiritual legs, begin to move me forward, in the name of Jesus.
192. I receive power, to operate three levels of locomotion; I shall walk, I shall run and I shall fly as an eagle, in the name of Jesus.
193. O Lord, lift me to the higher ground, in the name of Jesus.
194. I become unstoppable, as the wind, in the name of Jesus.
195. As from today, my middle name becomes excellence and advancement, in the name of Jesus.
196. Uncompleted projects in my life, receive the touch of God, in Jesus' name.
197. I subdue and overthrow, all the anti-progress forces, in the name of Jesus.
198. Evil strangers, flee away and never appear again, in the name of Jesus.
199. Every wicked device, against my life, receive frustration, in Jesus' name.
200. Every cloth of disgrace, I tear you to pieces, in the name of Jesus.

201. O God, who disgraced Ahitophel, bring the counsel of my enemies to nothing, in the name of Jesus.
202. You are the God of performance, perform wonders in my life, in the name of Jesus.
203. Oh Lord, make me a positive wonder, in the name of Jesus.
204. By the power of God, dark places shall not oppress me, in Jesus' name.
205. I cancel, every satanic appointment with death, in the name of Jesus.
206. I bury, every shrine conjuring my image, in the name of Jesus.
207. I am hot coals of fire, therefore any witchdoctor that tampers with my destiny, shall be roasted, in the name of Jesus.
208. Every witchcraft power, touching my life, die, in the name of Jesus.
209. I refuse, that my life be used as a sacrifice material to the devil, in the name of Jesus.
210. Every evil covenant, to my life, break now, in the name of Jesus.

SECTION CONFESSION

I tread upon and destroy completely all strongholds and barriers of the enemy against me, in the name of Jesus. I tread on them with the shoes of the gospel of the Lord Jesus Christ. I make an utter ruin of them all and all their possessions, kingdoms, thrones, dominions, palaces and everything in them, in Jesus' name. I erase them all and I make them completely desolate, in Jesus' name. My strength is in the Lord Jesus Christ, Jesus is my strength, I receive strength from the Lord, in the name of Jesus. The word of God says that He will restore to me, the years that the locust has eaten, the cankerworm, and the caterpillar, and the palmerworm, in the name of Jesus. With the blood of Jesus, the Lord will flush my land and wash my palms and possessions, in the name of Jesus. The whole world, may decide to go wild with evil flowing like a flood. The enemy, in his evil machinations, may decide against me. The earth may choose not to tremble; whatever may be or happen, I refuse to be shaken, in the name of Jesus.

MFM 2015 SEVENTY DAYS PRAYER & FASTING

I trust, in the word of God, the word stands sure when I speak it, it will accomplish the purpose for which I have spoken it, in Jesus' name. I am the manifestation, the product and the result of God's word. God has spoken into my life and I have become the manifested presence of Jehovah God on earth. I expressly manifest everything, the word of God says I am. I am filled with the word of life. Because the Lord disappointeth the devices of the crafty, so that their hands cannot perform their enterprise. Every work of the strong, the wicked, the evil and the enemy against my life, shall not prosper, in the name of Jesus. In the name of Jesus, I claim the power in the name of the Lord to overcome all the troops of the enemy. In the name of Jesus Christ, by the presence of God in my life, I command the wicked to perish before me; and melt away like wax in the fire. I am a child of God, I am dwelling in the secret place of the most high God, I am protected and covered under the shadow of the wings of Jehovah, in the name of Jesus.

SECTION VIGIL
(To be done at night between the hours of 12 midnight and 2am)
HYMN FOR THE VIGIL (Page 14)

1. O Lord, let the imagination of the wicked for our country be neutralized, in the name of Jesus.
2. Every secret I need to know, about my mother's lineage, be revealed, in the name of Jesus.
3. Every secret I need to know, about my hometown, be revealed, in Jesus' name.
4. Every secret I need to know, about the work I am doing, be revealed, in the name of Jesus.
5. Oh Lord, give unto me the Spirit of revelation and wisdom in the knowledge of Yourself.
6. Oh Lord, make your way plain before my face on this issue.
7. Oh Lord, remove spiritual cataract from my eyes.
8. Every organised worker of iniquity, depart from me, in the name of Jesus.

9. O Lord, let all my enemies be ashamed and sore vexed, in Jesus' name.
10. My Father, let sudden shame be the lot of all my oppressors, in Jesus' name
11. Every power, planning to tear my soul like a lion tears a lamb, be dismantled, in the name of Jesus.
12. God shall destroy the camp of the enemy, and their camp shall never be built up, in the name of Jesus.
13. O Lord, according to the deeds of the wicked, give them the works of their hands, in the name of Jesus.
14. O Lord, put off my sackcloth and gird me with gladness, in Jesus' name.
15. O Lord, cast out my enemies in the multitude of their transgressions, in Jesus' name.
16. Every organised worker of iniquity, depart from me, in the name of Jesus.
17. O Lord, let all my enemies be ashamed and sore vexed, in Jesus' name.
18. My Father, let sudden shame be the lot of all my oppressors, in Jesus' name
19. Every power, planning to tear my soul like a lion tears a lamb, be dismantled, in the name of Jesus.
20. God shall destroy the camp of the enemy, and their camp shall never be built up, in the name of Jesus.
21. O Lord, according to the deeds of the wicked, give them the works of their hands, in the name of Jesus.

SECTION 5 - BREAKING THE IDOL CHAINS

Scripture Reading: Exodus 20

Confession: Ezekiel 37:23 Neither shall they defile themselves any more with their idols, nor with their detestable things, nor with any of their transgressions: but I will save them out of all their dwelling places, wherein they have sinned, and will cleanse them: so shall they be my people, and I will be their God.

SECTION 5 DAY I (12-09-2015)

Reading through the Bible in 70 Days (Day 41 - Isaiah 6:13 - 30:8 Day 40 - Ecclesiastes 2:5-12:14; Song of Solomon 1:1- 8:14; Isaiah 1:1 - 6:12)
Devotional Songs (Pages 11-14)
Praise Worship
Prayer of Praise and Thanksgiving (Pages 15 & 16)

1. Every idol chain, holding me down, break, in the name of Jesus.
2. Negative anointing, of my family idols, clear away from my blood, in the name of Jesus.
3. Idols of my father's house, crying against my destiny, be silenced, in the name of Jesus.
4. Every idol power, barking against my full scale laughter, shut up and die, in the name of Jesus.
5. Every battle, provoked against my life, by family idols, scatter unto desolation, in the name of Jesus.
6. Agenda of idol powers, to paralyse my breakthroughs, die, in Jesus' name.
7. Tormenting powers, fashioned against me, by idol powers, release me and die, in the name of Jesus.
8. Wasters and emptiers assigned by idol powers to waste my life, die by fire, in the name of Jesus.

9. Every conscious and unconscious covenant, with any idol, break by fire, in the name of Jesus.
10. Yoke manufacturers, of the idol of my father's house, I damage your power, in the name of Jesus.
11. Arrows, fired into my destiny, by the idols in my foundation, die, in the name of Jesus.
12. Anger of heaven, provoked by my family idols, be cancelled by the blood of Jesus, in the name of Jesus.
13. Every evil dedication, that speaks against my moving forward, I dash you to pieces, in the name of Jesus.
14. Powers, mentioning my name on evil altars, be silenced and die, in the name of Jesus.
15. Every crooked line, drawn into my journey by idol power, be wiped off by the blood of Jesus, in the name of Jesus.
16. Any generational defect, sponsored by my family idol, clear away by the power in the blood of Jesus, in the name of Jesus.
17. Troubles, assigned against my life by idol powers, clear away by fire, in the name of Jesus.
18. Every shrine, mentioning my name, clear away by the power in the blood of Jesus, in the name of Jesus.
19. Every destiny miscalculation, provoked by idol powers, be reversed, in the name of Jesus.
20. Pursing powers, of my father's house, turn back and roast, in Jesus' name.
21. I recover, all my divine opportunities wasted by the family idols, in the name of Jesus.

SECTION 5 DAY 2 (13-09-2015)

Confession: Ezekiel 37:23 Neither shall they defile themselves any more with their idols, nor with their detestable things, nor with any of their transgressions: but I will save them out of all their dwelling places, wherein they have sinned, and will cleanse them: so shall they be my people, and I will be their God.

Reading through the Bible in 70 Days (Day 42-   Isaiah 30:9 - 50:7)
Devotional Songs (Pages 11-14)
Praise Worship
Prayer of Praise and Thanksgiving (Pages 15 & 16)

22. Every vagabond anointing, contributed into my life by my foundational idols, clear away, in the name of Jesus.
23. Every evil oil, poured on my head by the idols of my father's house, clear away, in the name of Jesus.
24. Cross road powers, and evil sacrifice powers, lose your power, in Jesus' name.
25. Rough places, prepared for my life's journey by family idols, break to pieces, in the name of Jesus.
26. Every open or hidden name, that serves as a ladder of affliction, be cancelled by the blood of Jesus, in the name of Jesus.
27. I vomit by fire, any thing I have consumed from the table of darkness, in the name of Jesus.
28. Satanic regulators, using foundational idolatry as a ladder against me, die, in the name of Jesus.
29. Every evil flow, into my life from foundational idolatry, dry up by the blood of Jesus, in the name of Jesus.
30. Every limitation, introduced into my journey by foundational idol power, roast, in the name of Jesus.
31. I retrieve my blessings, from the grip of any shrine or altar, in Jesus' name.

32. I jump out, of the valley of death sponsored by idol powers, in Jesus' name.
33. Every connection, between foundational idolatry and my dream life, break by fire, in the name of Jesus.
34. Any idol power, calling for my sacrifice in order to demand worship, die, in the name of Jesus.
35. Serpents and scorpions, of my father's house, lose your powers, in the name of Jesus.
36. Dark markets, sponsored by idol powers to sell my virtues, close down, in the name of Jesus.
37. Lord, cut down the idols of my father's house, in the name of Jesus.
38. O Lord, let the idols of my father's house, be confounded and their images and powers, broken to pieces, in the name of Jesus.
39. I renounce, all idolatry in my blood line, in the name of Jesus.
40. I break, all curses of idolatry in my blood line, in the name of Jesus.
41. O Lord, sprinkle Your water upon me and wash me clean from all pollution of idolatry, in the name of Jesus.
42. Every chain of idolatry, binding my destiny, break to pieces, in Jesus' name.

SECTION 5 DAY 3 (14-09-2015)

Confession: Ezekiel 37:23 Neither shall they defile themselves any more with their idols, nor with their detestable things, nor with any of their transgressions: but I will save them out of all their dwelling places, wherein they have sinned, and will cleanse them: so shall they be my people, and I will be their God.

Reading through the Bible in 70 Days (Day 43- Isa 50:8-66:24; Jer 1:1-6:24)
Devotional Songs (Pages 11-14)
Praise Worship
Prayer of Praise and Thanksgiving (Pages 15 & 16)

43. Every dedication, made by my ancestors before any idol to cage my future, I break that dedication by the power in the blood of Jesus
44. I release my name, I release my virtue, from the yoke and dominion of idolatry, in the name of Jesus.
45. Every curse of idolatry, afflicting my ancestral line, be broken, in Jesus' name.
46. Every evil river, flowing into my life from any form of idolatry, dry up, in the name of Jesus.
47. Every oath, every promise, every covenant, made by my ancestors before any idol, break now, in the name of Jesus.
48. Holy Ghost fire, break every chain of ancestral idolatry from my life, in the name of Jesus.
49. My Father, my Father, my Father, let every Goliath in my ancestry fall down and die, in the name of Jesus.
50. My Father, my Father, my Father, let every Pharaoh in my ancestry, fall down and die, in the name of Jesus.
51. My Father, my Father, my Father, let every Herod in my ancestry, fall down and die, in the name of Jesus.
52. My Father, my Father, my Father, let every Sennacherib in my ancestry, fall down and die, in the name of Jesus.
53. My Father, my Father, my Father, uphold me and recover my glory from the chains of idolatry, in the name of Jesus.
54. My Father, my Father, my Father, soak the totality of my life, in the blood of Jesus and free me from every chain and shackle of idolatry, in Jesus' name.
55. Every agenda, of idol worshippers for my life, be cancelled, in Jesus' name..
56. Every yoke of idiolatry, troubling my destiny, be cancelled, in Jesus' name.
57. Father, arise by Your power and glory, deliver my family from collective captivity, in the name of Jesus.
58. My Father, my Father, my Father, uphold me and deliver me from the aroma and aura of idolatry, in the name of Jesus.

59. Any promissory note, written by my ancestors before any idol, I tear them up, in the name of Jesus.
60. Any agreement, between my ancestors and any idol, I break that agreement, in the name of Jesus.
61. I renounce, every demonic name attached to me and my family, in the name of Jesus.
62. I dissociate my life, from every name given to me under satanic anointing, in the name of Jesus.
63. I break the flow, of any evil river coming into my life through these unprofitable names, in the name of Jesus.

SECTION 5 DAY 4 (15-09-2015)

Confession: Ezekiel 37:23 Neither shall they defile themselves any more with their idols, nor with their detestable things, nor with any of their transgressions: but I will save them out of all their dwelling places, wherein they have sinned, and will cleanse them: so shall they be my people, and I will be their God.

Reading through the Bible in 70 Days (Day 46: Jeremiah 6:25-25:23)

Devotional Songs (Pages 11-14)

Praise Worship

Prayer of Praise and Thanksgiving (Pages 15 & 16)

64. I refuse, to come under the control and domination of any satanic name, in the name of Jesus.
65. Every witchcraft name, be dissolved from my fore-head and navel, in the name of Jesus.
66. I receive, the seal of the Holy Spirit upon my life, in Jesus' name.
67. Every hidden or silent name, given to me to destroy my destiny on my naming ceremony day, I nullify you, in Jesus' name.

68. I take back, all the grounds given to Satan by my ancestors, in Jesus' name.
69. I apply the blood of Jesus, to break all consequences of parental sins in the name of Jesus.
70. I release myself, from the umbrella of any collective captivity, in the name of Jesus.
71. I release myself, from any inherited bondage, in the name of Jesus.
72. O Lord, send Your axe of fire, to the foundation of my life and destroy every evil plantation.
73. Blood of Jesus, flush out from my system, every inherited satanic deposit, in the name of Jesus.
74. I release myself, from the grip of any problem transferred into my life from the womb, in the name of Jesus.
75. I break and loose myself, from every collective evil covenant, in the name of Jesus.
76. I vomit, every evil consumption that I have been fed with as a child, in the name of Jesus.
77. I command, all foundational strongmen attached to my life to be paralyzed, in the name of Jesus.
78. Any rod of the wicked, rising up against my family line, be rendered impotent for my sake, in the name of Jesus.
79. I cancel, the consequences of any evil local name attached to my person, in the name of Jesus.
80. I refuse, to drink from the fountain of sorrow, in Jesus name.
81. I release myself, from the bondage of evil altars, in the name of Jesus. Say this once, then be repeating, "I release myself, in the name of Jesus." Spend some time on this.

82. I cancel, every demonic dedication, in the name of Jesus. Be repeating, "I cancel you, in the name of Jesus."
83. Every evil altar, erected against me, be disgraced, in the name of Jesus.
84. Anything done against my life, under demonic anointing be nullified, in the name of Jesus.

SECTION 5 DAY 5 (16-09-2015)

Confession: Ezekiel 37:23 Neither shall they defile themselves any more with their idols, nor with their detestable things, nor with any of their transgressions: but I will save them out of all their dwelling places, wherein they have sinned, and will cleanse them: so shall they be my people, and I will be their God.

Reading through the Bible in 70 Days (Day 45-   Jeremiah 25:24-43:4)
Devotional Songs (Pages 11-14)
Praise Worship
Prayer of Praise and Thanksgiving (Pages 15 & 16)

85. I curse, every local altar fashioned against me, in the name Jesus.
86. Every evil priest, ministering against me at any evil altar, receive the sword of God, in the name of Jesus.
87. Every stubborn evil altar priest, drink your own blood, in the name of Jesus.
88. I release myself, from every satanic blood covenant, in the name of Jesus.
89. Every demonic padlock and chain, used against me in the dark world, catch fire and cut to pieces, in the name of Jesus
90. I release myself, from every negative subjection to anything or person, in the name of Jesus.
91. Every evil tie, evil links, evil bonds, projected to manipulate my life, catch fire, in the name of Jesus.

92. I repent, from all ancestral idol worship, in the name of Jesus.
93. My enemies, shall not rejoice over me, in the name of Jesus.
94. Keep me as the apple of thy eyes, hide me under the shadow of thy wings, O Lord, in the name of Jesus.
95. O Lord, barricade me from the wicked that oppress me and from my deadly enemies who compass me about, in the name of Jesus.
96. Arise, O Lord, disappoint my oppressors and cast them down, in Jesus' name.
97. O Lord, deliver my soul from the wicked with thy sword, in the name of Jesus.
98. I will call upon the Lord, who is worthy to be praised, so shall I be saved from mine enemies, in the name of Jesus.
99. O God, send out Your arrows and scatter the oppressors, in the name of Jesus.
100. O God, shoot out your lightning and discomfit them, in the name of Jesus.
101. O Lord, let the smoke go out of Your nostrils, and fire out of Your mouth, to devour all plantations of darkness in my life, in the name of Jesus.
102. O God, thunder from heaven against all my oppressors, in the name of Jesus.
103. O Lord, with the blast of Your nostrils, disgrace every foundational bondage, in the name of Jesus.
104. O God, deliver me from my strong enemy, which hated me for they are too strong for me, in the name of Jesus.
105. O God, bring down every high look, that is downgrading my potentials, in the name of Jesus.

SECTION 5 DAY 6 (17-09-2015)

Confession: Ezekiel 37:23 Neither shall they defile themselves any more with their idols, nor with their detestable things, nor with any of their transgressions: but I will save them out of all their dwelling places, wherein they have sinned, and will cleanse them: so shall they be my people, and I will be their God.

MFM 2015 SEVENTY DAYS PRAYER & FASTING

Reading through the Bible in 70 Days (Day 46-Jeremiah 43:5-52:34; Lamentations 1:1-5:3)

Devotional Songs (Pages 11-14)

Praise Worship

Prayer of Praise and Thanksgiving (Pages 15 & 16)

106. I receive power, to run through satanic troop, in Jesus' name.
107. I receive power, to leap over every demonic wall of barrier, in Jesus' name.
108. O Lord, teach my hands to war, in the name of Jesus.
109. Every bow of steel, fashioned by the enemy, break by my hands, in the name of Jesus.
110. Every covenant, with the earth against my life, break, in the name of Jesus.
111. Every covenant, with the sun, moon, and stars against my life, break, in the name of Jesus.
112. Every covenant, with the water against my life, break, in the name of Jesus.
113. I apply the blood of Jesus, to break the power of any idol over my life. Sing this song: "There is power mighty in the blood (2ce). There is power mighty in the blood of Jesus Christ. There is power mighty in the blood."
114. O Lord, turn all the evils directed at me to good, in the name of Jesus.
115. I command, all powers of evil directed at me to return directly to the sender, in the name of Jesus.
116. God, make everything the enemy has said is impossible in my life, possible, in the name of Jesus.
117. I release myself, from the umbrella of any collective captivity, in Jesus' name.
118. I release myself, from any inherited bondage, in the name of Jesus.
119. Blood of Jesus, flush out from my system, every inherited satanic deposit in the name of Jesus.
120. I release myself, from the grip of any problem transferred into my life from the womb, in the name of Jesus.

121. Blood of Jesus, and the fire of the Holy Ghost, cleanse every organ in my body, in the name of Jesus.
122. I break and loose myself, from every collective evil covenant, in Jesus' name.
123. I break and loose myself, from every collective curse, in the name of Jesus.
124. I vomit, every evil consumption I have been fed with as a child, in the name of Jesus.
125. I command, all foundational strongmen attached to my life to be paralysed, in the name of Jesus.
126. Any rod of the wicked, rising against my family line, be rendered impotent for my sake, in the name of Jesus.

SECTION 5 DAY 7 (18-09-2015)

Confession: Ezekiel 37:23 Neither shall they defile themselves any more with their idols, nor with their detestable things, nor with any of their transgressions: but I will save them out of all their dwelling places, wherein they have sinned, and will cleanse them: so shall they be my people, and I will be their God.

Reading through the Bible in 70 Days (Day 47 - Lamentations 5:4-5:22; Ezekiel 1:1 - 19:8)

Devotional Songs (Pages 11-14)
Praise Worship
Prayer of Praise and Thanksgiving (Pages 15 & 16)

127. I cancel, the consequences of any evil local name attached to my person, in the name of Jesus.
128. Pray aggressively against the following roots of collective captivity. Pray as follows; Every effect of ___ (pick from the underlisted one by one), upon my life, come out with all your roots, in the name of Jesus.
    - Evil physical design   - Evil dedication   - Parental curses

MFM 2015 SEVENTY DAYS PRAYER & FASTING

- Demonic marriage
- Envious rivalry.
- Demonic sacrifice
- Demonic incision
- Inherited infirmity
- Dream pollution
- Evil laying on of hands
- Demonic initiation
- Wrong exposure to sex
- Demonic blood transfusion
- Exposure to evil diviners
- Demonic alteration of destiny
- Fellowship with local idols
- Fellowship with family idols
- Destructive polygamy
- Fellowship with demonic consultants
- Unscriptural conception

129. Kolanut idols, hear the word of the Lord, clear away, in the name of Jesus.
130. Cowry idols, hear the word of Lord, clear away, in the name of Jesus.
131. Crossroad idols, hear the word of the Lord, clear away, in the name of Jesus.
132. Masquerade idols, hear the word of 'the Lord, clear away, in Jesus' name.
133. Marriage idols, hear the word of the Lord, clear away, in the name of Jesus.
134. Calabash idols, hear the word of the Lord, clear away, in the name of Jesus.
135. Poison of idols, in my blood, die, in the name of the Jesus.
136. Every dog, of my family idol, barking at my progress die, in Jesus' name.
137. Idol powers, assigned to waste my destiny die, in the name of Jesus.
138. Idol powers, behind my problems die, in the name of Jesus.
139. Every evil dedication, speaking against my destiny, die by the blood of Jesus.
140. My Father, I need help, help me, in the name of Jesus.
141. Evil spiritual parents, I bind you today, in the name of Jesus.
142. Every evil harvest, scatter by fire, in the name of Jesus.
143. Every destructive ancestral promise, made for my sake, die, in Jesus' name.
144. Blood of Jesus, arise in your power, purge my roots, in the name of Jesus.
145. Every visitation of darkness, melt away, by the thunder of God, in the name of Jesus.
146. Harvest of iniquity, of my father's house, die, by the blood of Jesus.

147. Harvest of iniquity, of my mother's house, die, by the blood of Jesus.

SECTION 5 DAY 8 (19-09-2015)

Confession: Ezekiel 37:23 Neither shall they defile themselves any more with their idols, nor with their detestable things, nor with any of their transgressions: but I will save them out of all their dwelling places, wherein they have sinned, and will cleanse them: so shall they be my people, and I will be their God.

Reading through the Bible in 70 Days (Day 48- Ezekiel 19:9 - 34:20)
Devotional Songs (Pages 11-14)
Praise Worship
Prayer of Praise and Thanksgiving (Pages 15 & 16)

148. Every territorial bondage, over my destiny, die, in the name of Jesus.
149. Every foundational power, summoning me to the bottom, die, in the name of Jesus.
150. O Lion of Judah, arise and destroy every foundational serpent and scorpion, in the name of Jesus
151. Foundational poverty yokes, break, in the name of Jesus.
152. Foundational witchcraft yoke, die, in the name of Jesus.
153. Thou power, of magnetic backwardness, die, in the name of Jesus.
154. Mantle of favour and breakthrough, fall on me, in the name of Jesus.
155. Every foundational power, challenging my destiny, die, in the name of Jesus.
156. Every power, of the idols of my father's house, die, in the name of Jesus.
157. Every idol, of my father's house, lose your hold over my life, in Jesus' name.
158. Arrows of sickness, originating from idolatry, loose your hold, in Jesus' name.
159. My Father, send Your angels, to bring each member of my family out of darkness into light, in the name of Jesus.

160. Thou power of my family idol, die, in Jesus' name.
161. Every angry altar, of my father's house, crying against my breakthrough, die, in the name of Jesus.
162. Every idol, seeking demotion of my destiny, die, in Jesus' name.
163. Every family cage, sponsored by idols, break, in Jesus' name.
164. Every evil chain, linking me to family idol, break, in Jesus' name.
165. My name, hear the word of the Lord; Depart from every evil altar, in the name of Jesus.
166. Every evil power, of my family idol, die, in the name of Jesus.
167. I withdraw my name, from every evil altar, in the name of Jesus.
168. My life, receive deliverance from every cage of idolatry, in the name of Jesus.

SECTION 5 DAY 9 (20-09-2015)

Confession: Ezekiel 37:23 Neither shall they defile themselves any more with their idols, nor with their detestable things, nor with any of their transgressions: but I will save them out of all their dwelling places, wherein they have sinned, and will cleanse them: so shall they be my people, and I will be their God.

Reading through the Bible in 70 Days (Day 49- Ezekiel 34:21-48:35; Daniel 1:1 - 2:19)

Devotional Songs (Pages 11-14)

Praise Worship

Prayer of Praise and Thanksgiving (Pages 15 & 16)

169. Thou power of God, shatter every agenda of foundational idolatry, designed against my life, in the name of Jesus.
170. I retire by fire, every occult priest divining against me, in the name of Jesus.
171. Every strange fire, prepared by family idols, die, in Jesus' name.

MFM 2015 SEVENTY DAYS PRAYER & FASTING

172. By the power in the blood of Jesus, I renounce the gods that my ancestors or I have served, that have brought me into collective captivity, in Jesus' nmae.
173. Every seed of idolatry, in my foundation, die, in Jesus' name.
174. The voice of my family idol, will not prevail over my destiny, in Jesus' name.
175. Every grip, of the evil consequences of the ancestral worship of my forefathers' god, over my life and ministry, break by fire, in Jesus' name.
176. Every unconscious evil soul-tie and covenant, with the spirits of my dead grandfather, grandmother, occult uncles, aunties, custodians of family gods/oracles/shrines, break, by the blood of Jesus.
177. Every decision, vow or promise, made by my forefathers contrary to my divine destiny, loose your hold by fire, in Jesus' name.
178. Every generational curse of God, resulting from the sin of idolatry of my forefathers, loose your hold, in the name of Jesus.
179. Every ancestral evil altar, conspiring against me, be dashed against the Rock of Ages, in the name of Jesus.
180. Every evil ancestral placenta manipulation, of my life, be reversed, in the name of Jesus.
181. Every ancestral life pattern, designed for me through vows, promises and covenants, be reversed, in the name of Jesus.
182. Every ancient gate of my place of birth, locking up my progress, hear the word of the Lord, lift up your heads and open, in the name of Jesus.
183. Every evil power, of my place of birth, die, in the name of Jesus.
184. I fire back, every arrow of my family idols, in the name of Jesus.
185. Every covenant, made with any family idol on my behalf, break by the blood of Jesus.
186. I break and cancel, every covenant with any idol and the yokes attached to it, in the name of Jesus.
187. Every landlord spirit, troubling my destiny, be paralysed, in the name of Jesus.

188. Every outflow, of satanic family name, die, in the name of Jesus.
189. I recover, every benefit, stolen by idol powers, in the name of Jesus.

SECTION 5 DAY 10 (21-09-2015)

Confession: Ezekiel 37:23 Neither shall they defile themselves any more with their idols, nor with their detestable things, nor with any of their transgressions: but I will save them out of all their dwelling places, wherein they have sinned, and will cleanse them: so shall they be my people, and I will be their God.

Reading through the Bible in 70 Days (Day 50-Daniel 2:20-12:13; Hosea 1:1-9:13)

Devotional Songs (Pages 11-14)

Praise Worship

Prayer of Praise and Thanksgiving (Pages 15 & 16)

190. Where is the God of Elijah, arise, disgrace every family idol, in the name of Jesus.
191. Every satanic priest, ministering in my family line, be retrenched, in the name of Jesus.
192. Arrows of affliction, originating from idolatry, loose your hold, in the name of Jesus.
193. Every influence, of idol worship, in my life, die, in the name of Jesus.
194. Every network, of idol power in my place of birth, scatter, in Jesus' name.
195. Every satanic dedication, that speaks against me, be dismantled by the power in the blood of Jesus.
196. I vomit, every food with idolatrous influence that I have eaten, in the name of Jesus.
197. Every unconscious evil internal altar, roast, in the name of Jesus.

198. Any stone of hindrance, constructed by family idol, be rolled away, in the name of Jesus.
199. The voice of foundational idols, will never speak again, in Jesus' name.
200. Every strongman, assigned by the idols of my father's house against my life, die, in the name of Jesus.
201. Every satanic promissory note, issued on my behalf by my ancestors, be reversed, in the name of Jesus.
202. Garments of opposition, designed by ancestral idols, roast, in the name of Jesus.
203. Every satanic cloud upon my life, scatter, in the name of Jesus.
204. My glory, buried by family idols, come alive by fire, in the name of Jesus.
205. Thou power of strange gods, legislating against my destiny, scatter, in the name of Jesus.
206. Idols of my place of birth, I break your chain, in the name of Jesus.
207. Thou vagabond power, assigned against me, die, in the name of Jesus.
208. I puncture, the imagination of oppression targeted at me, in Jesus' name.
209. Though an host should encamp against me, my heart shall not fear, in the name of Jesus. I receive the power to pursue and overtake my enemies, in the name of Jesus.
210. My enemies are wounded, they are unable to rise, they are fallen under my feet, in the name of Jesus.

SECTION CONFESSIONS

In the name of Jesus Christ, I hand over all my battles to the Lord Jesus Christ, the Lord fights for me and I hold my peace. I am an overcame through the name of Jesus Christ. I am victorious in all circumstances and situations that are against me, in Jesus' name. Jesus Christ has defeated all my enemies, and they are brought down and fallen under my feet, in the name of Jesus. I crush them all to the ground and I command them to begin to lick up the dust of the earth under my feet; for at the name of Jesus, every knee must bow, in the name of Jesus. When I call upon the name of the Lord, He shall stretch forth His mighty hand and lift me up above all my enemies and deliver me from all of them, in the name of Jesus.

May the Lord God to whom vengeance belongs pelt their rank, files and strongholds with His stones of fire, in the name of Jesus. I raise a dangerous high standard of the flood of the blood of Jesus against their re-enforcement, and I command all the encamped and advancing enemy troops to be roasted by fire, in the name of Jesus. I possess the gate of my enemies and with the blood of Jesus, I render their habitation desolate, in the mighty name of Jesus Christ.

SECTION VIGIL
(To be done at night between the hours of 12 midnight and 2am)
HYMN FOR THE VIGIL (Page 14)

1. Father, fight against them that fight against me, in the name of Jesus.
2. Father, take hold of my shield and buckler and stand up for my help.
3. O God, prepare the instruments of death against my enemies, in Jesus' name.
4. O God, ordain Your arrows, against my persecutors, in the name of Jesus.
5. O Lord, let every pit dug by the enemy, become a grave for the enemy, in Jesus' name.
6. You enemies of this country, dig your hole and dig it well, because, you will fall into it, in the name of Jesus.
7. Acidic prayer stones, locate the forehead of the Goliath of this country, in the name of Jesus.
8. Candle of the wicked, I put you out, quench, in the name of Jesus.
9. All information, stored in the caldron against me, catch fire, in Jesus' name.
10. I release, panic and havoc upon any gathering summoned to disgrace me, in Jesus' name.

11. I release. confusion and backwardness upon every satanic programmer attacking my star, in the name of Jesus.
12. Every cage, formed to imprison my star, I smash you, in Jesus' name.
13. I release, the ten plagues of Egypt upon every coven tormenting my existence, in the name of Jesus.
14. O Lord, make the devices of my adversaries of none effect, in Jesus' name.
15. O Lord, let them be clothed, with shame and dishonour that magnify themselves against me, in the name of Jesus.
16. Father, let not the foot of pride, come against me, in Jesus' name.
17. Thou, that exalteth thine self as an eagle against me, I knock you down, in Jesus' name.
18. Every ancestral debt collector, be silenced, in the name of Jesus.
19. Every locker and warehouse, holding my blessings of wealth, catch fire, in Jesus' name.
20. Invisible wall of barriers, stagnating my destiny, scatter, in Jesus' name.
21. Invisible barricades, stagnating my goals, scatter, in the name of Jesus.

SECTION 6 -
BREAKING THE YOKE OF DESTINY IMPOTENCE

Scripture Reading: John 17

Confession: Isaiah 60: 1 -2 Arise, shine; for thy light is come, and the glory of the Lord is risen upon thee. For, behold, the darkness shall cover the earth, and gross darkness the people: but the Lord shall arise upon thee, and his glory shall be seen upon thee.

SECTION 6 DAY I (22-09-2015)

Reading through the Bible in 70 Days (Day 51-Hosea 9:14-14:9; Joel 1:1 -3:21; Amos 1:1-9:15; Obadiah 1:1-1:21; Jonah 1:1-4:11; Micah 1:1-7:1)

Devotional Songs (Pages 11-14)

Praise Worship

Prayer of Praise and Thanksgiving (Pages 15 & 16)

1. I recover my destiny, from the grip of destiny robbers and manipulators, in the name of Jesus.
2. My life, become too hot for the enemy to handle, in the name of Jesus.
3. Every horn, pressing down the glory of my life, scatter, in the name of Jesus.
4. Lord, let the precious blood of Jesus, cleanse my life from the evil effects of past immoral life, in the name of Jesus.
5. I renounce, every anti-breakthrough habit in my life, in the name of Jesus.
6. Heavenly surgeons, do all necessary surgical operation in my life, for my breakthrough to manifest, in the name of Jesus.
7. Wherever my glory is tied, thunder fire of God, loose them now, in the name of Jesus.
8. Where is the Lord God of Elijah, arise and enlarge my coast by fire, in the name of Jesus.

9. Every spirit, of detained and delayed blessings, I cast you out of my life, in the name of Jesus.
10. Every hidden ancestral and blood covenants, hindering my prosperity, break, in the name of Jesus.
11. Every demonic monitoring gadget, assigned against my prosperity, scatter, in the name of Jesus.
12. Every evil monitoring eye, monitoring my prosperity for destruction, catch fire, in the name of Jesus.
13. Arise O God, and let the enemies of my prosperity scatter, in Jesus' name.
14. Every yoke of poverty, break by the blood of Jesus, in the name of Jesus.
15. My destiny, hear the word of the Lord, your time of weeping has expired, bring forth glory by fire, in the name of Jesus.
16. Every marine spirit, assigned against my prosperity, scatter, in Jesus' name
17. Every serpentine spirit, assigned against my prosperity, scatter, in Jesus' name.
18. Every night caterer, assigned against my prosperity, scatter, in Jesus' name.
19. You eaters of flesh and drinkers of blood, feeding on my prosperity, die, in the name of Jesus.
20. Every strongman, hindering my prosperity, fall down and die, in Jesus' name.
21. Every evil power, projecting into my dreams, fall down and die, in Jesus' name.

SECTION 6 DAY 2 (23-09-2015)

Confession: Isaiah 60: 1 -2 Arise, shine; for thy light is come, and the glory of the Lord is risen upon thee. For, behold, the darkness shall cover the earth, and gross darkness the people: but the Lord shall arise upon thee, and his glory shall be seen upon thee.

Reading through the Bible in 70 Days (Day 52-Micah 7:2-7:20; Nahum 1:1-3:19; Habakkuk 1:1- 3:19; Zephaniah 1:1- 3:20; Haggai 1:1-2:23; Zechariah 1:1-14:21; Malachi 1:1-2:6)

MFM 2015 SEVENTY DAYS PRAYER & FASTING

Devotional Songs (Pages 11-14)
Praise Worship
Prayer of Praise and Thanksgiving (Pages 15 & 16)

22. Any material, from my body, being used against my prosperity, catch fire, in the name of Jesus.
23. I nullify, premature and still-birth breakthrough, in the name of Jesus.
24. I release my destiny, from any witchcraft cage, in the name of Jesus.
25. I release my destiny, from any evil padlock, in the name of Jesus.
26. I release my destiny, from any evil chain, in the name of Jesus.
27. My destiny, hear the word of the Lord, arise and shine, in the name of Jesus.
28. Thou power of failure, at the edge of breakthrough in my life, break, in the name of Jesus.
29. Spirits of failure, at the edge of breakthrough, loose your hold upon my life, in the name of Jesus.
30. Every satanic poison, in my body, be neutralized by the blood of Jesus.
31. My spirit man, receive strength to bring forth glory, in the name of Jesus.
32. I fire back, every arrow of death, in the name of Jesus.
33. Every blood covenant, speaking against my destiny, break, in Jesus' name.
34. O Lord, if my life is not functioning well, correct it with the blood of Jesus
35. I withdraw, every power, that is in charge of poverty in my life, in Jesus' name.
36. Every spirit of failure, in my life, be destroyed, in the name of Jesus.
37. Every spirit of barrenness of good things in my life, be destroyed and be replaced with the spirit of abundant goodness, in the name of Jesus.
38. Every spirit of poverty, be destroyed and be replaced with the spirit of prosperity, in the name of Jesus.
39. Every power, that has desired to put me into shame, be destroyed by the blood of Jesus.

40. I destroy, any power that is in charge of destroying good things in my life, in the name of Jesus.
41. Any power, siphoning my blessings, lose your hold, in the name of Jesus.
42. Blood of Jesus, arise in Your bulldozing power, sanitize my destiny, in the name of Jesus.

SECTION 6 DAY 3 (24-09-2015)

Confession: Isaiah 60: 1 -2 Arise, shine; for thy light is come, and the glory of the Lord is risen upon thee. For, behold, the darkness shall cover the earth, and gross darkness the people: but the Lord shall arise upon thee, and his glory shall be seen upon thee.

Reading through the Bible in 70 Days (Day 53-Malachi 2:7-4:7; Matthew 1:1-13:13)

Devotional Songs (Pages 11-14)

Praise Worship

Prayer of Praise and Thanksgiving (Pages 15 & 16)

43. Holy Ghost fire, sanitize my life for supernatural prosperity, in Jesus' name.
44. O Lord, by the power that answereth Jabez, visit my life by fire, in Jesus' name.
45. Creative power of God, repair any damage done to my life and destiny structures, in the name of Jesus.
46. O God, arise and advertise Your creative power in my life, in the name of Jesus.
47. I pull down, the stronghold of barrenness of good things in the name of Jesus.
48. Every witchcraft power, bewitching my life, fall down and die, in Jesus' name.
49. O Lord, by Your power which knows no impossibility, let my glory manifest, in the name of Jesus.
50. This month, shall not pass me by; I must bring forth glory, in the name of Jesus.
51. My Father, bring forth signs and wonder in my life, in the name of Jesus.

52. I invite the power of God, into every department of my life, in Jesus' name.
53. Healing power of God, flow into my spirit man, in the name of Jesus.
54. I call forth my glory, from any captivity, in the name of Jesus.
55. Every clinical prophecy, covering my situation, be over-turned by fire, in the name of Jesus.
56. Where is the Lord God of Elijah, give me the miracle of supernatural prosperity, in the name of Jesus.
57. My Father, speak life and productiveness into my life, in the name of Jesus.
58. Every evil hand, laid on my destiny, catch fire, in the name of Jesus.
59. O God of deliverance, deliver me from every generational liability, in the name of Jesus,
60. I release my life, from the grip of evil plantations, in the name of Jesus.
61. I reject, every arrow assigned to torment my life, in the name of Jesus.
62. My head, life, destiny and blood, receive the fire of deliverance, in Jesus' name.
63. Every tree, that the enemy has planted against my prosperity, be uprooted by fire, in the name of Jesus.

SECTION 6 DAY 4 (25-09-2015)

Confession: Isaiah 60: 1 -2 Arise, shine; for thy light is come, and the glory of the Lord is risen upon thee. For, behold, the darkness shall cover the earth, and gross darkness the people: but the Lord shall arise upon thee, and his glory shall be seen upon thee.

Reading through the Bible in 70 Days (Day 54-   Matthew 13:14 - 24:39)
Devotional Songs (Pages 11-14)
Praise Worship
Prayer of Praise and Thanksgiving (Pages 15 & 16)

64. Every witchcraft decision, on my prosperity, be cancelled by fire, in the name of Jesus.
65. O God of prosperity, bring honey out of the rock for me, in the name of Jesus.
66. Any problem, that came into my life through past feeding from the table of the devil, receive solution, in the name of Jesus.
67. Any problem, that came into my life through ungodliness, receive solution, in the name of Jesus.
68. Any problem, that came into my life through the deposits of spirit wife/husband, be resolved by fire, in the name of Jesus.
69. Any problem, that came into my life through evil spiritual surgery, be resolved by fire, in the name of Jesus.
70. Every power, assigned to embarrass me maritally, I kill you now, in the name of Jesus.
71. My Father, let me experience the glory power of Jehovah, in the name of Jesus.
72. Holy Ghost fire, incubate my head, life and destiny for productivity, in the name of Jesus.
73. Any power, stealing from my body, catch fire, in the name of Jesus.
74. Every glory, that has departed from my life, return by fire, in the name of Jesus.
75. My Father, arise and advertise Your power in my life, in the name of Jesus.
76. I arise by fire, and possess my possessions of prosperity, in the name of Jesus.
77. My Father, bombard me with the anointing for prosperity, in Jesus' name.
78. Holy Ghost fire, arise, burn away every anti-prosperity infirmity, in the name of Jesus.
79. I speak destruction, unto any mountain of disappointment in my life, in the name of Jesus.
80. I speak death, unto any mountain of disgrace in my life, in the name of Jesus.
81. I speak paralysis, unto every mountain of embarrassment, in Jesus' name.

82. I decree civil war, against every company of the wicked, working against my life, in the name of Jesus.
83. O God, arise and release the earthquake of deliverance to deliver me, in the name of Jesus.
84. My destiny, receive deliverance by fire, in the name of Jesus.

SECTION 6 DAY 5 (26-09-2015)

Confession: Isaiah 60: 1 -2 Arise, shine; for thy light is come, and the glory of the Lord is risen upon thee. For, behold, the darkness shall cover the earth, and gross darkness the people: but the Lord shall arise upon thee, and his glory shall be seen upon thee.

Reading through the Bible in 70 Days (Day 55-Matthew 24:40 - 28:20; Mark 1:1 - 6:33)

Devotional Songs (Pages 11-14)

Praise Worship

Prayer of Praise and Thanksgiving (Pages 15 & 16)

85. I reject, every long-term or short-term poverty, in the name of Jesus.
86. Every satanic deposit, contrary to prosperity, in my body and in my family pattern, be flushed out, in the name of Jesus.
87. Every witchcraft padlock, used against my destiny, catch fire, in Jesus' name.
88. Holy Ghost fire, melt away any obstacle hindering my prosperity, in the name of Jesus.
89. My Father, locate the source of my problem and scatter it, in Jesus' name.
90. By the blood of Jesus, I cancel every negative report against my prosperity, in the name of Jesus.
91. Any damage, done to my destiny, receive healing, in the name of Jesus.
92. Father, expose every secret, responsible for delay of my prosperity, in the name of Jesus.

93. O Lord, incubate my destiny with Your fire, in the name of Jesus.
94. Every evil covenant, working against my prosperity, be neutralized by the blood of Jesus.
95. Thou enemy from my mother/father's house, responsible for delayed blessing in my life, receive the judgement of fire, in the name of Jesus.
96. Thou enemy from unfriendly friends, responsible for delay of my prosperity, be condemned by fire, in the name of Jesus.
97. Every evil water, washing away my breakthroughs, dry up, in Jesus' name.
98. Every curse of poverty, in my lineage, I neutralize you in my life, in Jesus' name.
99. Any power, that needs to die, for me to become what God has purposed for me to become, fall down and die, in the name of Jesus.
100. O God of Hananiah, Mishael, and Azariah, visit me by fire, in Jesus' name.
101. My destiny, receive divine fertilization this month, in the name of Jesus.
102. This year will not elude me, I receive grace to prosper, in the name of Jesus.
103. The power, that creates the heaven and earth, create my glory supernaturally, in the name of Jesus.
104. I refuse to waste money, on useless projects and investments in the name of Jesus.
105. Great and awesome glory, surround my life, in the name of Jesus.

SECTION 6 DAY 6 (27-09-2015)

Confession: Isaiah 60: 1 -2 Arise, shine; for thy light is come, and the glory of the Lord is risen upon thee. For, behold, the darkness shall cover the earth, and gross darkness the people: but the Lord shall arise upon thee, and his glory shall be seen upon thee.

Reading through the Bible in 70 Days (Day 56-   Mark 6:34 - 16:11)
Devotional Songs (Pages 11-14)

MFM 2015 SEVENTY DAYS PRAYER & FASTING

Praise Worship

Prayer of Praise and Thanksgiving (Pages 15 & 16)

106. O Lord, give me miracle testimonies to the glory of Your name, in the name of Jesus.
107. Father, correct anything that is wrong with my foundation, in Jesus' name.
108. Every demonic power energizing failure at the edge of my breakthrough, loose your hold, in the name of Jesus.
109. Every arrangement in the heavenlies, contending with my prosperity, break, in the name of Jesus.
110. Every stone of darkness or satanic animals, destroying my glory and breakthroughs, die in the name of Jesus.
111. Strong east wind of the Lord, blow against the Red Sea in my destiny now, in the name of Jesus.
112. O Lord, fight against the destroyer working against my increase and prosperity, in the name of Jesus.
113. Thou power of the desert, come out of my life and destiny now, in the name of Jesus.
114. O Lord, overthrow every programme of household witchcraft, assigned against my prosperity, in the name of Jesus.
115. I will see the great work of the Lord as He delivers my glory safely, in the name of Jesus.
116. Every negative horse and rider, in my destiny, be thrown into the sea of forgetfulness, in the name of Jesus.
117. O Lord, send Your thunder before me to drive non-productivity from my life and destiny, in the name of Jesus.
118. I cast out, every power casting out my glory, in the name of Jesus.
119. I shall not bring forth glory to murderers, in the name of Jesus.
120. Every power of murderers, be shattered, in the name of Jesus.

121. Every violence of dead glory, stop permanently, in the name of Jesus.
122. You evil star, causing ungodliness, die, in the name of Jesus.
123. I am loosed, from every oppression of ungodliness, in the name of Jesus.
124. I decree, the death of spirit husband/wife that is killing my glory, in the name of Jesus.
125. O Lord, help me to conquer the power of evil clinical prophesy, in the name of Jesus.
126. O Lord, give me wings of a great eagle to escape from failure at the edge of breakthroughs, in the name of Jesus.

SECTION 6 DAY 7 (28-09-2015)

Confession: Isaiah 60: 1 -2 Arise, shine; for thy light is come, and the glory of the Lord is risen upon thee. For, behold, the darkness shall cover the earth, and gross darkness the people: but the Lord shall arise upon thee, and his glory shall be seen upon thee.

Reading through the Bible in 70 Days (Day 57-Mark 16:12 - 16:20; Luke 1:1 - 9:27)

Devotional Songs (Pages 11-14)

Praise Worship

Prayer of Praise and Thanksgiving (Pages 15 & 16)

127. Every power, that has swallowed my glory, vomit them by fire, in the name of Jesus.
128. Every foundation of non-productivity, receive the judgement of God, in the name of Jesus.
129. I command, every evil plantation to drop off my destiny, in Jesus' name.
130. Every low self esteem, be converted to full self esteem, in the name of Jesus.
131. I confess every sin, my ancestors and I have committed, in the name of Jesus.

132. Lord, use the truth to purge me of iniquities (mention any known sin like disagreements, nagging, discouragement, unfaithfulness, ingratitude, etc).
133. O Lord, let the fire of Holy Ghost, fall on me and let it consume every deposit of darkness that hinders my prosperity, in the name of Jesus.
134. O Lord, judge every one that has vowed that I will not make it, in the name of Jesus.
135. Holy Ghost, let my destiny receive revival power, in the name of Jesus.
136. O Lord, disturb every attack on my glory, in the name of Jesus.
137. Holy Ghost fire, arrest and consume every power of failure at the edge of breakthrough, in the name of Jesus.
138. O Lord, let my body system receive power of healing and renewal, in the name of Jesus.
139. O Lord, I retrieve all of my property, which the enemy is using to stop my prosperity, in the name of Jesus.
140. Holy Ghost fire, loose my destiny, from the cage of water and witchcraft spirits, in the name of Jesus.
141. Holy Ghost fire, neutralize every projected food in my dream, that is working against my prosperity, in the name of Jesus.
142. O Lord, I desire a supernatural breakthrough, in the name of Jesus.
143. Lord Jesus, send the Holy Ghost on errand, to retrieve any of my property in the warehouse of the strongman, in the name of Jesus.
144. Holy Ghost, be merciful upon me this month, in the name of Jesus.
145. My glory, be loosed where you are tied, the Lord needs them, in Jesus' name.
146. It is time, O Lord, work in my family, the world is waiting to see Your glory in my life, in the name of Jesus.
147. I bind and cast out to the sea of forgetfulness, you spirit of destiny blockage, in the name of Jesus.

MFM 2015 SEVENTY DAYS PRAYER & FASTING

SECTION 6 DAY 8 (29-09-2015)

Confession: Isaiah 60: 1 -2 Arise, shine; for thy light is come, and the glory of the Lord is risen upon thee. For, behold, the darkness shall cover the earth, and gross darkness the people: but the Lord shall arise upon thee, and his glory shall be seen upon thee.

Reading through the Bible in 70 Days (Day 58-   Luke 9:28 - 19:41)
Devotional Songs (Pages 11-14)
Praise Worship
Prayer of Praise and Thanksgiving (Pages 15 & 16)

148. O Lord, let fire burn all demonic watchers and monitors, that have been delegated against my family, in the name of Jesus.
149. O Lord, arise and let all the enemies of my family scatter, in Jesus' name.
150. My destiny, tied inside the tree, depth of Atlantic Ocean, wind, rock or second heaven, come forth by fire, in the name of Jesus.
151. O Lord, let all my enemies be bound, and be in deep sleep until I give birth to my promised miracles, in the name of Jesus.
152. Every demonic agent, that is fighting against my glory, be frustrated by the blood of Jesus.
153. Every power, that has desired to put me to shame, be destroyed by the blood of Jesus.
154. Every power, that is sucking the fruit of my destiny, be consumed by the fire of the Holy Ghost, in the name of Jesus.
155. Every spirit of failure, in my life be destroyed, in the name of Jesus.
156. I reject, every garment of poverty prepared for my life, in the name of Jesus.
157. I shall not miss, my time of visitation for prosperity, in the name of Jesus.
158. Lord Jesus, have mercy on me. If there is anything the devil still holds against me, to block my breakthroughs, forgive me and cleanse me by Your blood.

159. Before this time next year, I will be a bigger bundle of testimonies, in the mighty name of Jesus.
160. All weapons, fashioned against my testimony shall not prosper, in the name of Jesus.
161. You devil, loose your hold upon my destiny, in the name of Jesus.
162. From now on, let no man trouble me, for I bear in my body the marks of the Lord Jesus Christ.
163. From now on, let no ancestral power trouble me, and let no power from my father's house disturb my prosperity, in the name of Jesus.
164. From now on, let no marine power trouble my destiny, and let no disease trouble my destiny, in the name of Jesus.
165. By the bulldozing power of the Holy Ghost, I command every hindrance to prosperity in my life to die, in the name of Jesus.
166. Every disturbance and blockage, physical or spiritual, in my destiny, or anywhere in my system, get out, in the name of Jesus.
167. Every power, behind my delayed blessing, get out now, in the name of Jesus.
168. Every curse, working against blessing in my life, break, in the name of Jesus.

SECTION 6 DAY 9 (30-09-2015)

Confession: Isaiah 60: 1 -2 Arise, shine; for thy light is come, and the glory of the Lord is risen upon thee. For, behold, the darkness shall cover the earth, and gross darkness the people: but the Lord shall arise upon thee, and his glory shall be seen upon thee.

Reading through the Bible in 70 Days (Day 59-Luke 19:42 - 24:53; John 1:1 - 5:6)
Devotional Songs (Pages 11-14)
Praise Worship
Prayer of Praise and Thanksgiving (Pages 15 & 16)

169. Every contrary hand-writing, assigned against my blessing, wither, in the name of Jesus.
170. Every curse, issued against me, by satanic agent, backfire, in Jesus' name.
171. I release myself, from any inherited problem, in the name of Jesus.
172. Every bewitchment, assigned against my life and destiny, die, in the name of Jesus.
173. O God, arise and send Your angels to retrieve my glory from every satanic hiding place, in the name of Jesus.
174. By the power that established the heaven and the earth, let this month be my month of breakthroughs, in the name of Jesus.
175. You serpent, that attacks testimonies, and causes failure at the edge of breakthroughs, release me, in the name of Jesus.
176. Every problem, introduced into my life, by my past sexual sins, vanish, in the name of Jesus.
177. All the consequences, of sexual relationship with demonised partners, be removed from my life, in the name of Jesus.
178. All the consequences, of bewitched certificate, be cancelled, in Jesus' name.
179. Any material, in my body, presently in the dark kingdom, and is being used against my prosperity, cash fire, in the name of Jesus.
180. Every ungodly soul-tie, with all sexual partners of the past, break, in the name of Jesus.
181. This year, all those who have looked down on me because of my condition, shall laugh with me, in the name of Jesus.
182. I receive deliverance, from the spirit of monthly anxiety and nervousness, in the name of Jesus.
183. By the power, in the blood of Jesus, my expectations shall not be cut off, in the name of Jesus.
184. I retrieve, my original life and destiny, by force, in the name of Jesus.

185. I recover my normal destiny, from where it is hidden, in the name of Jesus.
186. Every decay in my life and destiny, come alive, in the name of Jesus.
187. Every contrary spiritual and physical verdict, pertaining to prosperity in my life, I cancel and neutralise you, in the name of Jesus.
188. O Lord, transform my destiny to the ones that will supernaturally achieve a successful prosperity, in the name of Jesus.
189. I retrieve my prosperity, by fire, in the name of Jesus.

SECTION 6 DAY 10 (01-10-2015)

Confession: Isaiah 60: 1 -2 Arise, shine; for thy light is come, and the glory of the Lord is risen upon thee. For, behold, the darkness shall cover the earth, and gross darkness the people: but the Lord shall arise upon thee, and his glory shall be seen upon thee.

Reading through the Bible in 70 Days (Day 60-   John 5:7 - 13:30)
Devotional Songs (Pages 11-14)
Praise Worship
Prayer of Praise and Thanksgiving (Pages 15 & 16)

190. Thou power of memory loss, die, in the name of Jesus.
191. Thou power of financial failure, die, in the name of, in the name of Jesus.
192. I soak my destiny, in the blood of Jesus.
193. I break, every witchcraft curse and spell concerning my destiny, in the name of Jesus.
194. Every power, stealing prosperity from my destiny, I bind and cast you out, in the name of Jesus.
195. O Lord, let Your creative anointing, restore my destiny and glory, in the name of Jesus.
196. O doors of prosperity, open unto me, in the name of Jesus.

197. The anointing, that openeth the doors of the prosperity and breakthrough, fall upon me, in the name of Jesus.
198. Every strongman, attached to the gate of my destiny, fall down and die, in the name of Jesus.
199. O Lord, let the doors of my destiny be opened by fire, in Jesus' name.
200. Fire of the God of Elijah, pass through my destiny and burn to ashes, everything that is contrary to prosperity, in the name of Jesus.
201. By the power, that directed angel Gabriel to Zachariah, let the angel of my miracle testimony locate me now, in the name of Je
202. O Lord, send Your fire to the foundation of my problems, in Jesus' name.
203. Every evil plant in my destiny be destroyed by the blood of Jesus, in the name of Jesus.
204. I retrieve, by fire and the blood of Jesus, every personal effect in the camp of the wicked, being used to manipulate my life and glory, in Jesus' name.
205. In the name of Jesus, I declare that my life and destiny system, is in a perfect working condition.
206. I reject, reverse and revoke, every curse of poverty in my life and glory, in the name of Jesus.
207. I evacuate by fire, every evil deposit and plantation upon my destiny, in the name of Jesus.
208. O Lord, take away every shame, reproach, confusion and frustration from me and heap it upon all my enemies, in the name of Jesus.
209. O Lord, turn my sorrows to joy, my pains to gain and my mockery to celebration, in the name of Jesus.
210. I cancel, with the blood of Jesus, every evil blood covenant entered into by myself, parents, ancestors, in the name of Jesus.

MFM 2015 SEVENTY DAYS PRAYER & FASTING

SECTION CONFESSIONS

In the name of Jesus, I am inscribed in the palm of God's mighty hand, I am neatly tucked away and hidden from all the evils and troubles of this present world, in the name of Jesus. Henceforth, I refuse to live in fear. Rather, my fear and dread shall be upon all my enemies. As soon as they hear of me, they shall submit themselves to me, in Jesus' name. God wishes above all things that I prosper, in Jesus' name. I receive prosperity, in Jesus' name. God has not given me the spirit of bondage, to fear. The word of God, is quick and powerful in my mouth. God has put the power of His word in my mouth, in the name of Jesus. I am not a failure, I shall operate at the head only and not beneath, in the name of Jesus.

I totally trust in the Lord, and I am not leaning on my own understanding. I fill my heart with the words of faith; I receive and speak the words of faith. The young lions do lack, and suffer hunger; but I who seeks the Lord God Almighty, shall not lack any good thing, in the name of Jesus. God is my strong Rock and my House of defence, in the name of Jesus. In the name of Jesus Christ, I hand over all my battles to the Lord Jesus Christ, the Lord fights for me and I hold my peace. The Lord has bowed down His righteous ears, to deliver me speedily, in the name of Jesus. I shall eat the riches of the Gentiles, and in their glory I shall boast myself, and all shall see and shall acknowledge that I am the seed, which the Lord has blessed.

SECTION VIGIL

(To be done at night between the hours of 12 midnight and 2am)
HYMN FOR THE VIGIL (Page 14)

1. Every secret I need to know, about my environment, be revealed, in Jesus' name.
2. Every secret I need to know, about my father's lineage, be revealed, in the name of Jesus.
3. O wind of God, drive away every power of the ungodly, rising against our country, in the name of Jesus.

4. O Lord, let the rage of the wicked, against our country be rendered impotent, in the name of Jesus.
5. O God arise, and give me the neck of my enemies, that I might destroy those who hate me, in Jesus' name.
6. By God's power, my enemies will cry, but there will be none to deliver them, in the name of Jesus.
7. I receive power, to beat my aggressors to smallness as the dust before the wind, in the name of Jesus.
8. Oh Lord, reveal to me every secret behind this particular issue whether beneficial or not.
9. Every counsel of evil kings against our country, scatter, in Jesus' name.
10. My Father, break the teeth of the ungodly in this nation, in Jesus' name.
11. You enemies of our country, fall by your own counsel, in Jesus' name.
12. Holy Spirit, reveal deep and the secret things to me about . . . , in Jesus' name.
13. My Father, break the teeth of the ungodly, in Jesus' name.
14. I receive power, to operate with sharp spiritual eyes that cannot be deceived, in the name of Jesus.
15. Bow down Thine ear to me, O Lord, and deliver me speedily, in Jesus' name.
16. O Lord, pull me out of every hidden net of the enemy, in Jesus' name.
17. My times are in Your hand, deliver me from the hands of my enemies and from those who persecute me, in the name of Jesus.
18. O Lord, let the wicked be ashamed, and let them be silent in the grave, in the name of Jesus.
19. Every lying lip, speaking against me, be silenced, in Jesus' name.
20. O Lord, bring the counsel of the ungodly to nought, in the name of Jesus.
21. I receive power, to operate with sharp spiritual eyes that cannot be deceived, in the name of Jesus.

MFM 2015 SEVENTY DAYS PRAYER & FASTING

SECTION 7 - PRAYERS FOR TERRITORIAL DELIVERANCE OVER YOUR AREA

Scripture Reading: Psalm 149

Confession: Prov. 3:33 The curse of the Lord is in the house of the wicked: but he blesseth the habitation of the just.

SECTION 7 DAY 1 (02-10-2015)

Reading through the Bible in 70 Days (Day 61-John 13:31 - 21:25; Acts 1:1 - 6:3)

Devotional Songs (Pages 11-14)

Praise Worship

Prayer of Praise and Thanksgiving (Pages 15 & 16)

1. Lord, I thank You, for Your power that is able to deliver, from every form of bondage and from every form of demonic oppression, in the name of Jesus.
2. As I go, into this level of warfare, I receive a covering of the blood of Jesus. I stay in the strong tower, which is the name of the Lord.
3. I receive, God's unction and power upon my tongue, in the name of Jesus.
4. I forbid, any satanic backlash or retaliation against me and my family, in the name of Jesus.
5. In this battle, I shall fight and win, I shall be a victor and not a victim, in the name of Jesus.
6. I put on, the helmet of salvation, the belt of truth, the breastplate of righteousness; I wear the shoe of the gospel and I take the shield of faith, as I go into this territorial intercession and warfare, in the name of Jesus.
7. I bind and rebuke, the princes and powers in charge of this (mention the name of the city), in the name of Jesus.
8. I command the fire of God, on all the idols, traditions, sacrifices and rituals on this land, in the name of Jesus.

MFM 2015 SEVENTY DAYS PRAYER & FASTING

9. I break, all the agreements made between the people of this city and satan, in the name of Jesus.
10. I dedicate and claim, this city for God, in the name of Jesus.
11. O Lord, let the presence, dominion, authority and blessings of God be experienced in this city, in the name of Jesus.
12. I destroy, and decree total removal of arsons, strikes, juvenile delinquencies, lawlessness, nakedness, pornography, immoralities, homosexualism and drug addiction in this city, in the name of Jesus.
13. I prophesy, against all the satanic altars in high places in this city, to be consumed by the fire of God, and their ashes blown away by the East wind, in the name of Jesus.
14. Every satanic altar, around this vicinity, become desolate and let all covenants being serviced by these altars be revoked and broken, in the name of Jesus.
15. You the sword and the hand of the Lord, be against the priests and priestesses ministering on all those satanic altars and high places, and let their places be found no more, in the name of Jesus.
16. I silence, every evil voice speaking from all satanic altars and high places of this city, in the name of Jesus.
17. All curses, brought about by ritual sacrifices and satanic tokens, be revoked, in the name of Jesus.
18. I paralyse, the evil powers of idolatrous priests of this city, in the name of Jesus.
19. I command the stars, the sun, the moon and the winds, to begin to fight against the diviners and astrologers, who have been using these elements, against the move of God in this city, in the name of Jesus.
20. You judgement of God, come upon the ancient and scornful men, who rule over this city by sorcery, satanic manipulation and witchcraft, in Jesus' name.
21. I deprogramme, whatever the enemy has programmed into the lives of the people of this city, in the name of Jesus.

MFM 2015 SEVENTY DAYS PRAYER & FASTING

SECTION 7 DAY 2 (03-10-2015)

Confession: Prov. 3:33 The curse of the Lord is in the house of the wicked: but he blesseth the habitation of the just.

Reading through the Bible in 70 Days (Day 62 - Acts 6:4 - 17:25)

Devotional Songs (Pages 11-14)

Praise Worship

Prayer of Praise and Thanksgiving (Pages 15 & 16)

22. By the blood of Jesus, I destroy every blood covenant made upon any satanic altar that has brought untold hardships unto the people of this city, in the name of Jesus.
23. I frustrate, the tokens of liars, and I make mad all diviners, enchanters and sorcerers who are operating at any altar against this city, in the name of Jesus.
24. I desecrate, every satanic altar in this city, by the blood of Jesus and cancel all their associated covenants, in the name of Jesus.
25. Every marine altar, in this city, catch fire, in the name of Jesus.
26. All territorial altars, in this city, catch fire, in the name of Jesus.
27. All astral altars, in this city, catch fire, in the name of Jesus.
28. You marine spirits, operating in this neighbourhood, be paralysed and suffocated, in the name of Jesus.
29. I break, every limitation brought about by the influence of satanic altars in this city, in the name of Jesus.
30. Every devoted land and evil forest, in this city be demolished, in Jesus' name.
31. By the power, in the name of our Lord Jesus Christ, I command the citadel of the wicked forces to shift base from this city, in the name of Jesus.
32. I prophesy, command, and decree, that the peace, glory, love, mercy of God be established in this city, in the name of Jesus.
33. O Lord, let the fear, righteousness, godliness, knowledge and wisdom of God be established in this city, in the name of Jesus.

34. O Lord, let there be repentance of hearts and hunger for God in this city, in the name of Jesus.
35. The gospel of the kingdom of God, shall no longer be restricted by any satanic altar or high places in this city, in the name of Jesus.
36. In the name of the Lord Jesus Christ, I declare a new day of divine visitation and deliverance for this city and its neighbourhood.
37. I prophesy, that new altars to Jehovah God will be raised in every household of this city, in the name of Jesus.
38. Henceforth, I declare that Jesus Christ is Lord over this city, in Jesus' name.
39. O Lord, let the presence of guardian angels be over my habitation 24 hours daily, in the name of Jesus.
40. O Lord, let the glorious light of God shine on my premises 24 hours daily, in the name of Jesus.
41. O Lord, let the particles of the soil and stone, in my premises, receive the fire of God and torment every evil presence in my compound, in the name of Jesus.
42. Every evil word, uttered or ordained by the owner, the builders and former occupants of where I'm living, die, in Jesus' name.

SECTION 7 DAY 3 (04-10-2015)

Confession: Prov. 3:33 The curse of the Lord is in the house of the wicked: but he blesseth the habitation of the just.

Reading through the Bible in 70 Days (Day 63-Acts 17:26 - 28:31; Romans 1:1 - 3:1)

Devotional Songs (Pages 11-14)

Praise Worship

Prayer of Praise and Thanksgiving (Pages 15 & 16)

43. Every demonic utterance, invocation, spell, charms, amulets, witchcraft burial in the house where I live, die, in the name of Jesus.

44. Every demonic operation, being carried out in the night against my habitation, scatter, in the name of Jesus.
45. Every occult covenant, binding on my habitation, be cancelled by the blood of Jesus.
46. Any power, using the sand to control my life, fall down and die, in Jesus' name.
47. You ground, vomit every enchantment against me, in the name of Jesus.
48. Any power, mixing incantations with the sand against me, fall by your sword, in the name of Jesus.
49. O God, as I release this sand, let it travel to every messenger of darkness working against my life and by this sand let every stubborn yoke in my life break, in the name of Jesus.
50. I bind and rebuke, the princes and powers in charge of my environment, in Jesus' name.
51. Fire of God, come upon all the idols, traditions, sacrifices and rituals in my environment, in Jesus' name.
52. I break, all the agreements made between the people of my environment and satan, in the name of Jesus.
53. I dedicate, and claim my environment for God, in the name of Jesus.
54. Every satanic altar around my environment, become desolate and let all covenants being serviced by these altars be revoked and broken, in the name of Jesus.
55. I silence, every evil mouth speaking from all satanic altars and high places of my environment, in Jesus' name.
56. All curses, brought about by ritual sacrifices and satanic token be revoked, in the name of Jesus.
57. Every marine altar, in my environment catch fire, in the name of Jesus.
58. All territorial altars, in my environment catch fire, in the name of Jesus.
59. I command, the citadel of the wicked forces to shift base from my environment, in the name of Jesus.

60. In the name of Jesus, I declare a new day of divine visitation and deliverance for my environment.
61. O Lord, arise and judge the seat of immorality in my neighborhood, in the name of Jesus.
62. Every form of hypnotism, working in my environment, I paralyse you, in the name of Jesus.
63. O Lord, let every enchantment and sorcery against me, not see the light of day, in the name of Jesus.

SECTION 7 DAY 4 (05-10-2015)

Confession: Prov. 3:33 The curse of the Lord is in the house of the wicked: but he blesseth the habitation of the just.
Reading through the Bible in 70 Days (Day 64-Romans 3:2 - 16:27; 1 Corinthians 1:1 - 4:3)
Devotional Songs (Pages 11-14)
Praise Worship
Prayer of Praise and Thanksgiving (Pages 15 & 16)

64. Father, arise and cut off, the spirit of divination in my neighborhood, in the name of Jesus.
65. Lord, let the bewitchment over my environment, be broken and let the instruments of such bewitchment lose their grip, in the name of Jesus.
66. Every object or animal, around me that facilitates witchcraft attack, I command you to receive God's fire of judgement, in the name of Jesus.
67. Lord, use me to judge witchcraft operations in my environment, in the name of Jesus.
68. I hold this dust now, O Lord. I put this dust into Your holy and mighty hands. Let this dust carry the electrocuting power and pursing power to sanitize my environment. Let every habitation of evil altars, covens, and vagabond evil powers be rendered desolate, in Jesus' name.

69. O Lord, let this dust, that I have released, render my habitation uninhabitable to eaters of flesh and drinkers of blood. Let this dust, travel under the thunder of Your power and destroy every agent and messengers of darkness working against my destiny, in the name of Jesus.
70. By this dust, I render every incantation and satanic utterance, made in my environment impotent, in the name of Jesus.
71. As long as these agents of darkness, will make contact with the ground, air, water and breath in air, let dust in the ground, air and water trouble them unto submission or destruction, in the name of Jesus.
72. As long as satanic consultants and contractors, will return to the dust, as long as they eat food brought out of the ground, let their divinations and survey backfire, in Jesus' name.
73. O wind, hear the word of the Lord, carry warfare back to the camp of environmental polluters, environmental witchcraft, environmental sorcerers, environmental familiar spirits, environmental robbers, environmental ritualists, environmental enchanters, environmental diviners, and environmental murderers, in the name of Jesus.
74. By this dust, let all handwriting of darkness, written against me and my family in darkness, be dismantled, in the name of Jesus. Let this dust, carry the weapons of war in heaven and evacuate Goliaths, Herods, Pharaohs, and Sennacheribs from my street, city and country by fire, by thunder and by force, in the name of Jesus.
75. I hold this sand, after the order of Moses, and I use it as a point of contact for the land from where it was removed; let every particle of this sand, become hot coals of fire to roast any deposit of darkness in my environment, in the name of Jesus.
76. O Lord, let this sand, carry judgement back to the camp of any negative cover over the land of my environment, in the name of Jesus.

77. O Lord, let the words that I programme into this sand now, become sharp arrows to pursue my pursuers and put my enemies to flight, in the name of Jesus.
78. After the order of Moses, let this sand bring judgement to magicians, sorcerers, and enchanters assigned against my place of dwelling, in the name of Jesus.
79. Any power, mixing incantations with the dust against me, fall by your sword, in Jesus' name.
80. O God, as I release this dust, let it travel to every messenger of darkness working against my life and by this dust let every stubborn yoke in my life break, in the name of Jesus.
81. Visualise that you are holding dust in your hand by faith now and begin to say, "I sprinkle the dust against you messengers of the darkness, in the name of Jesus.
82. I paralyse, all evil legs roaming about for my sake, in the name of Jesus.
83. I command every soil particle and stone, at the top and foundation of my house to become a consuming fire to torment every invisible demon in my life, in Jesus' name.
84. All that have been uttered and ordained by the builder, occupant or the land owner of the house(s) I have stayed in the past, and where I am now, the various demonic utterances, invocations, spells, including charms and amulets, buried, hung or hidden in the house, melt by the fire of the Holy Spirit, in the name of Jesus.

SECTION 7 DAY 5 (06-10-2015)

Confession: Prov. 3:33 The curse of the Lord is in the house of the wicked: but he blesseth the habitation of the just.

Reading through the Bible in 70 Days (Day 65-1 Corinthians 4:4 - 16:24; 2 Corinthians 1:1 - 5:3)

Devotional Songs (Pages 11-14)

MFM 2015 SEVENTY DAYS PRAYER & FASTING

Praise Worship

Prayer of Praise and Thanksgiving (Pages 15 & 16)

85. I soak, every grain of this sand that forms part of the soil of my dwelling place, in the Blood of Jesus.
86. I dislodge and bind, every evil mixture in the concrete of my dwelling place, in Jesus' name.
87. Father, let the blessings of heaven, fall like rain upon my dwelling place, in Jesus' name.
88. Holy Ghost Fire, incubate and take full control of my environment.
89. O Lord, let every particle of this sand, carry the fire and glory of God. Let the God of Elijah soak these sand particles in the power of the Holy Ghost. As these particles touch my environment, let them release favour, blessings, breakthroughs, new glorious things, opportunities, joy, salvation, glory, wisdom and enlargement upon my life and environment, in the name of Jesus.
90. O Lord, let them also release judgment, confusion, civil war, destruction, scattering, fire, thunder, paralysis, sword of the Lord, and violent angels, against every enemy of my life and environment, in the wonder working name of Jesus.
91. I soak, every grain of this sand that forms part of the soil of my dwelling place, in the blood of Jesus.
92. Any power, mixing incantations with the dust against me, fall by your sword, in Jesus' name.
93. O Lord, let the words that I programme into this sand now, become sharp arrows to pursue my pursuers and put my enemies to flight, in Jesus' name.
94. O God, as I release this dust, let it travel to every messenger of darkness working against my life, and by this dust let every stubborn yoke in my life break, in the name of Jesus.
95. O Lord, let this sand carry judgement back to the camp of any negative cover over the land of my environment, in the name of Jesus.

96. After the order of Moses, let this sand bring judgement to magicians, sorcerers, and enchanters assigned against my place of dwelling, in the name of Jesus.
97. O Lord, enlarge my coast beyond my wildest dream, in the name of Jesus.
98. Every dark power, afflicting my environment, scatter, in the name of Jesus.
99. I paralyse, all evil legs roaming about for my sake, in the name of Jesus.
100. Glorious light of God, shine on my premises, to become consuming fire and crush every dark presence in my environment, in the name of Jesus.
101. I destroy, every evil property and demonic operation in my house, in Jesus' name.
102. All occult covenants, binding on my dwelling place, be dissolved and rendered impotent, in the name of Jesus.
103. Network of witchcraft, operating in my environment, scatter, in Jesus' name
104. Every graveyard spirit, caging people in this environment, loose your hold, in the name of Jesus.
105. Thou power of silent oppression, operating in this environment, I bury your power, in the name of Jesus.

SECTION 7 DAY 6 (07-10-2015)

Confession: Prov. 3:33 The curse of the Lord is in the house of the wicked: but he blesseth the habitation of the just.
Reading through the Bible in 70 Days (Day 66-2 Corinthians 5:4 - 13:14; Galatians 1:1 - 6:18; Ephesians 1:1 - 5:20)
Devotional Songs (Pages 11-14)
Praise Worship
Prayer of Praise and Thanksgiving (Pages 15 & 16)

106. Every environmental prison, with dispossessing power, break, in the name of Jesus.

107. All virtues, that are buried under the earth, in my environment, I exhume you, by power and fire, in the name of Jesus.
108. Thou power, of environmental graveyards, die, in the name of Jesus.
109. Every environmental agenda, forcing princes to trek while servants are on the horses, be overturned, in the name of Jesus.
110. Holy Ghost fire, sanitize my environment by the power in the blood of Jesus.
111. Every inspiration of the devil, controlling my environment, be dissolved by fire, in the name of Jesus.
112. Every satanic dedication of lands, by ancestors, to the devil, I break that dedication, in the name of Jesus.
113. I remove, every cover of darkness upon the land, in the name of Jesus.
114. Thou land of my habitation, I set you free from every idol pollution, in the name of Jesus
115. Every altar, built on the land, that has brought a cover of darkness, scatter, in the name of Jesus.
116. Every power, that has worked over the land of my habitation, in the dark world, I recover you and be redeemed by the blood of Jesus.
117. Every band of wickedness, over my environment, break, in Jesus' name.
118. My neck, shall not be broken by territorial spirits, in the name of Jesus.
119. Blood, poured on the ground will not eat me up, in the name of Jesus.
120. Every charm buried in the ground to subdue my life, I destroy you, in the name of Jesus.
121. I quench, every anger energised through the land against me, in Jesus' name.
122. Every landlord spirit, troubling my health, be paralysed, in the name of Jesus.
123. Every government of darkness, upon the land of my habitation, be dismantled, in the name of Jesus.
124. O Lord, let the sanctifying power, of the blood of Jesus, move upon my environment, in the name of Jesus.

125. O Lord, let the purifying power, of the blood of Jesus, take control of my environment, in the name of Jesus.
126. Every evil spiritual occupant, of the land where I dwell, I bind you into the desert, in the name of Jesus.

SECTION 7 DAY 7 (08-10-2015)

Confession: Prov. 3:33 The curse of the Lord is in the house of the wicked: but he blesseth the habitation of the just.

Reading through the Bible in 70 Days (Day 67-Ephesians 5:21 - 6:24; Philippians 1:1 - 4:23; Colossians 1:1 - 4:18; 1 Thessalonians 1:1 - 5:28; 2 Thessalonians 1:1 - 3:18; 1 Timothy 1:1 - 5:5)

Devotional Songs (Pages 11-14)

Praise Worship

Prayer of Praise and Thanksgiving (Pages 15 & 16)

127. Every activity of witchcraft, upon my environment, I paralyse you and I disgrace you, in the name of Jesus.
128. Every strange visitation, upon the land of my habitation, I paralyse your power, in the name of Jesus.
129. Every evil consultation, of power of darkness, taking place in my environment, I silence you, in the name of Jesus.
130. Father, I agree with the word of the Lord, that every power causing strange activities in my environment, will be quenched, in the name of Jesus.
131. Every gate, of water spirits and occultic powers upon the land, be closed, in the name of Jesus.
132. All the high places, of water spirits upon the land, I bind you and pull you down, in the name of Jesus.
133. Every familiar spirit, operating in the land, I pull down your power, in the name of Jesus.

134. Every power, releasing sicknesses in my environment, carry your sicknesses and disappear, in the name of Jesus.
135. Every satanic whirlwind, stirred up in my environment, I bind your power, in the name of Jesus.
136. Every spiritual gate, upon this land, I pull you down, in the name of Jesus.
137. Every curse, of neglect upon this land, break, in the name of Jesus
138. Every curse, of suffering upon the land of my habitation, break, in the name of Jesus.
139. Every curse of waywardness upon the land of my habitation, break, in the name of Jesus.
140. Every curse of babel, which is division, upon the land of my habitation, be broken, in the name of Jesus.
141. Every curse of marital problem, upon the land of my habitation, break, in the name of Jesus.
142. Every curse of hardship, upon the land of my habitation, break, in the name of Jesus.
143. Every curse of spiritual and physical barrenness, upon the land of my habitation, break, in the name of Jesus.
144. Every curse and covenant of sickness, upon the land of my habitation, break, in the name of Jesus.
145. Every curse and covenant of strange happenings, upon the land of my habitation, break, in the name of Jesus.
146. Every curse of wickedness, upon the land of my habitation, break, in the name of Jesus.
147. Every curse of tragedy, upon the land of my habitation, break, in the name of Jesus.

SECTION 7 DAY 8 (09-10-2015)

Confession: Prov. 3:33 The curse of the Lord is in the house of the wicked: but he blesseth the habitation of the just.

Reading through the Bible in 70 Days (Day 68-1 Timothy 5:6 - 6:21; 2 Timothy 1:1 - 4:22; Titus 1:1 - 3:15; Philemon 1:1 - 1:25; Hebrews 1:1 - 11:40)

Devotional Songs (Pages 11-14)

Praise Worship

Prayer of Praise and Thanksgiving (Pages 15 & 16)

148. Every curse of hindrances, upon the land of my habitation, break, in the name of Jesus.
149. Every curse of backwardness, upon the land of my habitation, break, in the name of Jesus.
150. Every curse of failure, upon the land of my habitation, break, in Jesus' name.
151. Every curse of failure, at the edge of breakthrough, upon the land of my habitation, break, in the name of Jesus.
152. I overthrow, I bind, I destroy, the influence of occult powers upon this land, in the name of Jesus.
153. Father, let Your fire, deal with the witches and wizards upon this land, in the name of Jesus.
154. Every throne and caldron of darkness, upon the land, catch fire, in the name of Jesus.
155. Father, I stand as Your child, and I destroy the ability of the wicked upon this land, in the name of Jesus.
156. Every satanic veil, upon this land, catch fire, in the name of Jesus.
157. Every cloud of sin, upon the land of my habitation, break, in Jesus' name.
158. Every demonic covenant, and initiations upon this land, I break you and I pull you down, in the name of Jesus.
159. You powers of bondage, upon this land, I bury you now, in the name of Jesus.

160. Every spirit of divination and incantation, upon this land, I destroy your power, in the name of Jesus.
161. By the power in the blood of Jesus, I revoke the negative influences of charms, magic and sorcery upon this land, in the name of Jesus.
162. I call down, the judgement of God, upon the spirits that donated this land unto satan, in the name of Jesus.
163. Father, arise, track down the wicked in this land, and bring them to judgement, in the name of Jesus.
164. Father, arise, track the enemy of progress upon this land, and bring them to judgement, in the name of Jesus.
165. Every satanic alliance, to perpetuate injustice upon this land, scatter, in the name of Jesus.
166. Every landlord spirit, laying claims to this land, I paralyse your powers, in the name of Jesus.
167. Every backwardness, that has occurred upon the land of my habitation, be reversed and become progress, in the name of Jesus.
168. Holy Ghost arise, pass through the land of my habitation and disgrace the wicked, in the name of Jesus.

SECTION 7 DAY 9 (10-10-2015)

Confession: Prov. 3:33 The curse of the Lord is in the house of the wicked: but he blesseth the habitation of the just.

Reading through the Bible in 70 Days (Day 69-Hebrews 12:1 - 13:25; James 1:1 - 5:20; 1 Peter 1:1 - 5:14; 2 Peter 1:1 - 3:18; 1 John 1:1 - 5:21; 2 John 1:1 - 1:11)

Devotional Songs (Pages 11-14)

Praise Worship

Prayer of Praise and Thanksgiving (Pages 15 & 16)

169. Father, let the glory of the Lord, overshadow this land, in the name of Jesus.

170. I decree by the decree of heaven, that there will be peace around and within this place, in the name of Jesus.
171. By fire, by force, I buy this land back from every demonic owner, in the name of Jesus.
172. All curses, spells, jinxes and evil covenants operating on this land, I break you by the power of the Holy Spirit, in the name of Jesus.
173. Father, according to the order of Obed-Edom, reside here in this land, and give us divine breakthroughs, in the name of Jesus.
174. Father, let Your name be glorified upon this land, in the name of Jesus.
175. There will be no parking, waiting or tarrying of the devil on this land, in the name of Jesus.
176. Holy Ghost, incubate this land, and make it too hot for the enemy to dwell in, in the name of Jesus.
177. Father, let the wall of fire surround this place, in the name of Jesus.
178. From the foundation to the roof of this house, let there be divine immunity against infirmity, in the name of Jesus.
179. Father, make me to multiply and not diminish, physically, spiritually in every area of my life in this land, in the name of Jesus.
180. Every astral projection, of the wicked into this land, be rendered null and void, in the name of Jesus.
181. I close the door, of this land to all satanic ministers, diviners, enchanters and evil men, in the name of Jesus.
182. I reject, every agenda of the devil against me and against every occupant of this land, in the name of Jesus.
183. Father, be in-charge of this land as from now on, in the name of Jesus.
184. I revoke, any evil covenant that must have been made on this land, in the name of Jesus.
185. I command, all the demons behind such covenants to depart from this land, in the name of Jesus.

186. You the glory of the Lord, overshadow this land, in the name of Jesus.
187. Father, let Your mighty angels encamp round about this land, in Jesus' name.
188. I redeem this place, in the name of the Father, and of the Son and of the Holy Ghost, in the name of Jesus.
189. O God, arise and let the heavens be opened over this land, in Jesus' name.

SECTION 7 DAY 10 (11-10-2015)

Confession: Prov. 3:33 The curse of the Lord is in the house of the wicked: but he blesseth the habitation of the just.

Reading through the Bible in 70 Days (Day 70 -2 John 1:12 - 1:13; 3 John 1:1 - 1:14; Jude 1:1 - 1:25; Revelation 1:1 - 22:21)

Devotional Songs (Pages 11-14)

Praise Worship

Prayer of Praise and Thanksgiving (Pages 15 & 16)

190. I command every blanket of darkness, over this place to be removed, right now, in the name of Jesus.
191. I prophetically, draw this premises into a lasting covenant with the Lord Jesus Christ, in the name of Jesus.
192. Everything planted into this land, contrary to my peace, catch fire, in the name of Jesus.
193. Any coven or any evil association, meeting on this land, I chase you out, in the name of Jesus.
194. Father, arise in Your power, station Your angels of war all over my environment, in the name of Jesus.
195. Father, arise by the thunder of Your power and purge my habitation, in the name of Jesus.
196. I draw the circle of the blood of Jesus around my habitation, in Jesus' name.

197. O Lord, let every sand and particles of soil in this environment become hot coals of fire, that the enemy cannot access or trouble, in the name of Jesus.
198. O God, arise and let Your fire envelope this land, in the name of Jesus.
199. O God, arise and laminate this land, by the power in the blood of Jesus, in the name of Jesus.
200. O God, arise, move in an awesome way to bless this land, in Jesus' name.
201. Every satanic claim, upon the land of my habitation, I revoke you by the power in the blood of Jesus.
202. Strangers upon this land, flee unto desolation, in the name of Jesus.
203. Every sorcery, enchantment upon this land, break into pieces, in the name of Jesus.
204. Every witchcraft operation, and wizard anointing upon this land, be dissolved, in the name of Jesus.
205. You the land of my habitation, become too hot for the enemy, in the name of Jesus.
206. Father, station Your special angels, all over this land so that no power of the enemy can penetrate, in the name of Jesus.
207. Father, make it to happen so that anyone who steps upon this land, will experience the favour of God, in the name of Jesus.
208. Father, anything buried in the land of my habitation, that is causing trouble for this land, let Your angels set it ablaze, in the name of Jesus.
209. Every opportunity waster, upon this land, I bind and cast you out, in the name of Jesus.
210. Yokes and satanic padlocks, upon this land, catch fire, in the name of Jesus.

SECTION CONFESSIONS

I trample under my feet, every serpent of treachery, evil reports, accusations, machinations and criticisms, in the name of Jesus. In the time of trouble, the Lord my God and my Father shall hide me in His pavilion; in the secret places of His tabernacle shall He hide me. With an overrunning flood, will the Lord make an utter end of my enemy's habitation, in the name of Jesus. The Lord has sent the fear and the dread of me upon all my enemies, that the report or information of me shall cause them to fear, tremble and be in anguish, in the name of Jesus. I am of good cheer, and I believe in the sanctity and infallibility of God's word, in the name of Jesus. According to this time, it shall be said of me and my family, what God has done, in the name of Jesus. I therefore command all enemy troops arrayed against me to scatter, as I call down the thunder fire of God upon them, in the name of Jesus.

I shall no longer be disappointed, or fail at the edge of my desired miracles, success and victory, in the name of Jesus. It is written: behold, I and the children whom the Lord has given me are for signs and for wonders in Israel from the Lord of hosts which dwelleth in mount Zion. I stand upon this infallible word of God and claim every letter of its promises, in the name of Jesus. I also covenant myself and my household onto the Lord: my fruits, I shall dedicate and surrender to the blessings and pleasures of God who has blessed me and banished my reproach forever, in the name of Jesus. The Lord is my light and my salvation, whom shall I fear? The Lord is the strength of my life; of whom shall I be afraid? When the wicked, even mine enemies and foes, come upon me to eat up my flesh, they stumbled and fell, in the name of Jesus.

SECTION VIGIL
(To be done at night between the hours of 12 midnight and 2am)
HYMN FOR THE VIGIL (Page 14)

1. O Lord, put off my sack cloth and gird me with gladness, in Jesus' name.
2. Bow down Thine ear to me, O Lord, and deliver me speedily, in Jesus' name.
3. O Lord, pull me out of every hidden net of the enemy, in Jesus' name.
4. My times are in Your hand, deliver me from the hands of my enemies and from those who persecute me, in the name of Jesus.

5. O Lord, let the wicked be ashamed, and let them be silent in the grave, in the name of Jesus.
6. Every lying lip, speaking against me, be silenced, in Jesus' name.
7. O Lord, bring the counsel of the ungodly to nought, in the name of Jesus.
8. O Lord, deliver my soul from the sword and my destiny from the power of the dog, in the name of Jesus.
9. O God, arise by the thunder of Your power and save me from the lion's mouth, in the name of Jesus.
10. Thou power of the valley of the shadow of death, release my destiny, in the name of Jesus.
11. O gates blocking my blessings, be lifted up, in Jesus' name.
12. O Lord, keep my soul, let me not be ashamed and deliver me, in Jesus' name.
13. Every drinker of blood and eater of flesh coming against me, die, in the name of Jesus.
14. Though an host should encamp against me, my heart shall not fear, in the name of Jesus.
15. Evil, shall slay the wicked and they that hate the righteous shall be desolate, in the name of Jesus.
16. Father, fight against them that fight against me, in the name of Jesus.
17. Father, take hold of shield and buckler and stand up for my help, in the name of Jesus.
18. Father, draw out Your spear and stop my persecutors, in Jesus' name.
19. O Lord, let them be confounded and put to shame that seek after my soul, in the name of Jesus.
20. O Lord, let them be turned back and brought to confusion that device my hurt, in the name of Jesus.
21. O Lord, let the wicked be as chaff before the wind, and let the anger of the Lord chase them, in the name of Jesus.

Made in the USA
Lexington, KY
12 April 2016